THE WILD WEST SHOW

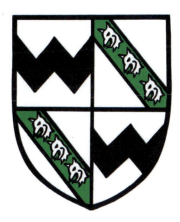

Cornwallis-West: Argent a fesse dancetty sable, for West, quartered with Argent a bend vert with three wolves' heads razed argent thereon, for Myddleton of Chirk.
(A History of the County of Hampshire Volume 5, (1912)

A STORY OF THE CORNWALLIS-WEST FAMILY

This edition published in 2009 by Natula Publications
Natula Ltd., Christchurch, Dorset BH23 1JD

Copyright © Raymond Curry 2009

The right of Raymond Curry to be identified as the author of this work has been asserted by him in accordance with the Copyright, Designs and Patent Act 1988.

ISBN 9781897887769

A CIP catalogue record of this book is available from the British Library.

All rights reserved. No part of this publication may be reproduced, stored in a retrieval system, or transmitted in any form or by any means (electronic, mechanical, photocopying, recording or otherwise) without the prior permission of the copyright holder.

Printed by Cpod, Trowbridge, Wiltshire.

Every attempt has been made by the Publisher to secure the appropriate permissions for the illustrations reproduced in this book, including where owners and copyright holders are different concerns.

If there has been any oversight we will be happy to rectify the situation. Written submission should be made to the Publisher.

All other illustrations, unless otherwise accredited, are from the author's or publisher's collections.

CONTENTS

	Page
ACKNOWLEDGEMENTS	v
INTRODUCTION	viii
1 The Fairy Tale and the Reality	1
2 Where it all began – Newlands Manor	4
Genealogy – The Cornwallis family	10
3 The Admiral – William Cornwallis	11
The Whitby family connection	31
4 The Captain – John Whitby	33
5 The Mother – Mary Anne Theresa	40
Genealogy – The West and Cornwallis-West families	47
6 The Ruthin Connection	48
7 The Daughter – Theresa	51
The Wild West Show	61
8 The Son – William	63
9 The Daughter in Law – Patsy	70
10 The Grandson – George	82
11 The Princess – Daisy	102
12 The Duchess – Shelagh	139
Genealogy – The Next Generations	144
The Hochberg / Pless family	145
13 The Great Grandson – Hansel	148
14 The Great Grandson – Lexel	167
15 The Great Grandson – Bolko	179
The Conclusion	183
Epilogue	192
Bibliography	194
Picture Acknowledgments	196

ACKNOWLEDGEMENTS

The picture of Admiral Sir William Cornwallis on the back cover, pages 10, 11 and in the pictorial genealogy is by R Gardner and was provided to the author by the 3rd Baron Cornwallis.

The pictures of William and Patsy Cornwallis-West in the pictorial genealogy and elsewhere, together with the pictures of Ruthin Castle on the cover and in the book are by kind permission of Anthony Saint Claire, Managing Director of Country Park Hotels.

The pictures of Captain Whitby and Mrs Theresa Whitby are in the ownership of the Hornyold-Strickland family of Sizergh Castle, Cumbria, to whom they were donated by George Cornwallis-West. I am very grateful to Mrs Hornyold-Strickland and her son for being allowed to use these two pictures of the couple as they seem to be the only ones known of them at that age. There do not appear to be any other pictures of John Whitby and only one or two others of his wife in her latter years. My thanks also go to the National Trust Staff at Sizergh Castle, for their assistance.

I am grateful to many other individuals for their kind assistance including:

Mithra Tonking, archivist at The Diocese of Lichfield for her help in tracing records within the Whitby family.

Staffordshire County Records for the copy of the register of birth date for John Whitby and the picture of Cresswell Hall.

The late Dr Colin White, former Director of the Royal Naval Museum, for his kind assistance in matters naval.

Mr Bob Braid, of the Milford-on-Sea Historical Record Society, for his considerable input and the lower picture on page 54 together with the picture of Daisy on page 104 which is in the possession of the society.

Mr Alan Chapple, of All Saints Parish Church Milford-on-Sea, who has kindly taken some of the pictures in the church.

Jacci Rhodes-Jury of Riverside, Milford-on-Sea, who was interrupted one day by the author but showed considerable interest in his endeavours, allowing pictures to be taken by him and later by Jane Martin of Natula Publications.

The residents of Newlands Manor have been kind enough to allow Jane Martin to take pictures of the house as it is today, and the author is grateful to Jane for her thoughtful observations on the draft put to her for consideration before publication.

W. John Koch in Canada, author of the biography on Princess Daisy and a considerable authority on her life, has been most helpful in his encouraging support, providing some pictures noted throughout the book and giving his good wishes for a successful publication.

The Director and staff, particularly Sylwia Smolarek, of the Muzeum Zamkowe w Pszczynie (Fürstenstein) in Poland for their help in providing pictures of Daisy, her husband Hans and his father, as well as Hansel and others, with permission for them to be included in this book.

The National Portrait Gallery for permission to use the picture of George Cornwallis-West on pages 62, 82 and in the pictorial genealogy.

I am, as ever, most grateful to Martin Blackman, my book finder, of Great Missenden, who manages to locate my various requests with remarkable speed.

In addition, the author is very indebted to his friend Geoff Smith, of Rotherham, who has helped by digging up various titbits of information, and suffering from the reading of copy about which he has made many helpful remarks, as well as taking pictures at Ruthin.

Lately Brian Jolly, who is researching and writing a work on the pictures at Sizergh Castle, has exchanged notes with the author about the Whitbys. This has been most useful and has assisted in clearing up a few points which have been modified in the copy. The author is very grateful for this cooperation. However, despite this exchange there are still some items of query to both parties and the author has decided to leave currently unresolved issues as such.

INTRODUCTION

During the writing of *Two Brothers Cornwallis* I became aware of the development of what one could only term as a 'new family', albeit one which had its roots in two of the oldest families who had served both King and country for many generations.

There have, no doubt, been many such alliances over the years, especially when British social orders were firmly established as 'upper' or 'lower'. The later ubiquitous 'middle' class was almost an invention of the 19th century, as in an extension of the industrial revolution many hoary hands were turned softer by the explosion of industries which enabled the enterprising to rise above their roots. More opportunities became available to the hard working, although it was not until the end of the 19th century that this change really took off.

The 20th century has seen further development so that what is now known as 'middle England' is a society of its own, with levels within its own ranks. The established social order with or without money, which was so important in the times of the people recounted in this book, has virtually gone, and it is has been replaced by a socio-economic grouping where wealth is largely the paramount objective at all levels.

To those born well prior to the Second World War there are some recollections, either direct or passed on from parents, of those earlier years; but to the present day family, results of the post war baby-boom, it is all a matter of history.

What has this digression about social orders to do with the forthcoming story, the reader may well ask?

The answer is that in the period which is covered by the lives of the Cornwallis-Wests, they went through that change, certainly in terms of position and prestige; indeed their finances also suffered as the ability to live off estate lands tenanted to others diminished year on year. Secondly, they found that positions of power changed from being gifts in the hands of the monarchies to bestow to being ones handed out by the newer 'democratically' elected governments or in some cases totalitarian regimes.

Thus, this family story is one very appropriate to the times, being quite typical of the changes occurring, especially in Europe.

In those former years, the 'double barrelled' surname was frequently associated with the desire to retain a family name when the last holder was a daughter about to marry, which act would normally put the old name to rest.

Within what might be called the parent family of Cornwallis that did happen, as a daughter married into the Wykeham Martin family, and a son of that link later changed his name by Royal assent to Cornwallis. Thus, the present 3rd Baron Cornwallis, who descends down that female bloodline, since his grandfather's ennoblement in 1927, holds the same titular name as his ancestor.

The Cornwallis-West name, which was to be so prominent for many years in the upper reaches of the aristocracy and Royal circles, was an invention to retain the name of a singular sailor who had not married, but whose 'adopted' family chose to remember his life. The West name was that of the family of Earl De La Warr, who had served from way back beyond Crécy; that of Cornwallis was also of considerable vintage. This link, however, was not one by blood; the lady who married into the West family and joined the two names had no real blood connection with Cornwallis, but she was one of some fortune, having been bequeathed the estates of the bachelor sailor, Admiral Sir William Cornwallis.

The development of this 'new' family was to be one which engaged society for some years, being closely involved with the rather light-hearted years of the Prince of Wales as he waited to assume the monarchy as Edward VII, and then up to and through the years of two world wars and the great social changes in that time.

Although the name Cornwallis–West is given as the true name of those who feature in this story, a fair amount of correspondence by others quoted in various books simply refers to them as West; both the Prince of Wales and the Duke of Westminster, for example, were writing to or about George West.

The lives of some descendants since that 19th century linking of the families are set out in the following pages, and a simple genealogical table of those who feature in this story is shown on the endpapers and in more detail on pages 9, 47 and 144.

There is no intention in this volume for it to be considered as a complete form of biography for any of the participants. In several instances, serious academic works about various family members have already exercised the literary talent of others. I am grateful for the information which is available in these books. They are listed in the Bibliography and are wholeheartedly recommended to readers whose appetite to know more is stimulated by this work.

So the purpose of this book is to try to relate in the form of a story the various characters in a series of essays, linking one to the other in a sequence by birth. Other books on the Cornwallis-Wests do not necessarily cover all the ground in that regard.

I have specifically avoided developing down the lines of the marriages beyond the ones whose lives were directly associated with the Cornwallis-West family. That would be beyond the intentions of the book. This story follows the family from its inception by an inheritance and the marriage of a young naval officer, then down the descendants of one part of the family.

Therefore any ongoing marriages and families such as arising from the sister of William Cornwallis-West, or the children of the marriage of Shelagh to Bend'Or the 2nd Duke of Westminster are not included, although the daughter of the latter couple, Ursula, has some mentions in respect of her support for Hans Pless during the period of his incarceration in World War Two.

The title of the book, *The Wild West Show*, arises from the name given to the family by Edward, the then Prince of Wales, particularly when they lived at Newlands because of their lively way of life. This was led by the ebullient Patsy, wife of William Cornwallis-West, and was replicated in her children, especially by the young Daisy.

The stories of the characters are individual, but some of the events covered in detail in a chapter may be referred to in another one about a related individual. This slight duplication is intended so that those who may read the book a chapter at a time can have some idea of consequential affairs.

Readers of this book who may be familiar with some of the people or places mentioned could be slightly confused by or query how some place or family names are presented within these pages. In order to explain some of the reasoning, a few cases and explanations are given:

The spelling of 'Guadaloupe' when referring to the ship of that name is used in the biography of the Admiral Cornwallis by George Cornwallis-West and is also the format in the navy list.

Various other names of people or places are affected by differing use of capital letters, and this is notable in the interpretations of De La Warr, or de la Warre. The latter, although used in the Admiral's biography, would appear to be a literal French translation. In fact over a period of many generations the presentation of the name has varied, even at one time being Delaware, from which the state in America was named. This change of presentation appears to be a transitional matter between the family generations and 'new beginnings'. Over the period from around 1761 and to date the usage has been De La Warr, so that is the variation used here as it ties in with the period of the story in these pages.

Other names of places and characters are given as taken straight from main primary sources of information: maps, documents or letters of the time such as Finisterre in Spain, Wurttemberg in Germany and the French Admiral being La Motte Piquet. The name of the ship *Belleisle*, of which John Whitby was the captain, is only one word.

Some names or places in Germany suffer from anglicised interpretations but that of the Grand Duke Mecklenburg-Strelitz is taken from a primary source.

There is a plethora of different spellings of the first name of Hans' second wife in various books: Clotilde, Clothilde, Clothilda and even Clotildita. The author has opted to use Clotilde as John Koch in his biography of Daisy, the first wife of Hans, refers to her as Clotilde de Silva y Gonzales de Candamo (of the Spanish House of the Marques de Arcicollar), which is abbreviated to Clotilde de Silva where appropriate.

There are several ways of writing the name of the owner of Newlands before Admiral Cornwallis: both D'Oyley and D'Oyly appear in a book published in 1832 and there are also references to d'Oyley and d'Oyly in other sources. The Milford Historical Society has Sir John Hadley D'Oyly on record as the previous owner, so we favour this spelling.

Regarding His Grace the 2nd Duke of Westminster, his *familia* of Bend'Or is used in his biography by George Ridley, a lifetime employee and friend of the Duke. The name derives from a racehorse owned by the family and is based on an historical incident which is described in Ridley's book.

Milford Barnes (Barns) and the other Milford manors are in various sources spelt with and without an 'e'; this book looks to the *History of the County of Hampshire Volume 5* for guidance.

The many books which have been written about Indian affairs have shown Tipu, Tippoo and other variations. That of Tippoo has been chosen for this book as being common in various sources.

ONE
THE FAIRY TALE

It could read almost like a fairy tale as once upon a time a rich man, who had never been married, befriended a younger married couple, treating them as his adopted son and daughter. In due course the young pair had a daughter and they all lived happily together. Unfortunately the young father then died of a sudden illness but the rich man continued to look after the lady he saw as his adopted daughter, and her child.

When the rich man died he left his house and estate to the young widowed mother and his money in trust for her young daughter. When the daughter became older she met and married a noble's grandson and their own child, a boy, was named after her benefactor. They inherited a big castle from the family of the noble's grandson, so they had two fine houses in which to live.

Their son in time inherited the castle and other estates and then married a beautiful lady, also from an old family. They had three children, one boy and two girls.

The father liked to stay at the castle and look after his estates, but he also worked hard at his offices including being a member of the Parliament and he had to go away on his duties. The mother loved to mix with the highest people in the land: nobles, ministers and even a Prince, the heir to the throne. She spent a lot of time at the other house where she often entertained the Prince and many other important people.

She helped her two daughters marry well, one to a Duke and the other to a Prince who lived far away in a huge castle in a foreign land. This daughter lived as a Princess and mixed with other Princes and even Kings. The son married an heiress, a widow older than himself.

So far this does seem to be a story from an ideal world, but sadly it was not to continue.

Although some members of the family were to remain close with each other, the others did not always see eye to eye with their relations. Indeed, amongst the three sons of the Princess there were to be many quarrels, and one of them died very young. Then a huge shift in social attitudes was to change their world. Two world wars intervened, and this divided the family even further because of the different countries in which they lived.

Some continued to live fairly comfortably, others lost much of their wealth as the world into which they had been born changed, never to be the same again. The Princess became very ill and was living in poverty when she died.

There is joy and sadness in this story, probably typical of many other families who lived through this period of great changes in the world, including the horror of two world wars.

Those at the upper end of society were largely deprived of their position but for others, who may have suffered the indignity of poverty for many generations, it was a chance of a new way of life which gave them fresh aspirations beyond their wildest dreams.

THE REALITY

This is the story of the Cornwallis-West family from 1835 until 1984 when it all ended, at least in that name.

The rich man was Admiral Sir William Cornwallis and his adopted family was Captain John Whitby and his wife Mary Anne Theresa.

These two officers first served together in the East India Station and thereafter for much of the time until the Battle of Trafalgar. John Whitby served as Flag Captain to the Admiral. They are the very foundation for this story about a family which had a significant impact in the early years of the 20th century.

The name Cornwallis-West was established on 20th March 1835 when a son, William, was born to Frederick Richard West, a grandson of the 2nd Earl De La Warr, and his second wife Theresa Whitby, the daughter of John and Mary Anne Theresa Whitby, whom he had married in 1827.

It is reputed that William was given the name Cornwallis as a Christian name, before the old family name of West, in order to comply with a condition of inheritance; but it is most likely that it was also because of the deep regard the young Theresa had for her benefactor whom she had known and revered since childhood. The act of creating the hyphenated surname did not in fact take place until some years had passed.

In due course, William married and had two daughters and one son whose lives traced an interesting picture in the years which bridged the huge change in social life at the turn of the 19th and 20th centuries. Some of the children of one daughter, who were born to riches and position, passed their later lives in relative obscurity.

However, before we continue with the story it would be useful to set the scene of the tale and the original friendship forged between the two naval officers.

The first of these two gentlemen was Admiral Sir William Cornwallis whose life is shortly to be set out. The following chapter gives some background on his home at Newlands Manor, near Lymington in Hampshire, where the story really starts.

The genealogical charts should assist understanding of the relationships between the people who make up this ongoing story of the Cornwallis-West family.

TWO

WHERE IT ALL BEGAN
NEWLANDS MANOR

In the area of South Hampshire between New Milton and Lymington, within the three manors of Milford, lies a house which was originally little more than a farmhouse until in 1798 the property was acquired by William Cornwallis from Sir John D'Oyly. At first he leased the property but then bought the freehold. For over a century that house was to be the subject of change and was for some time towards the end of that period to be the centre of social life in a fairly extreme form, at least for those days.

Newlands Manor lies to the West of the road to Everton from Milford-on-Sea, to the East of Barnes Lane just south of the A337, which is the road from Christchurch to Lymington.

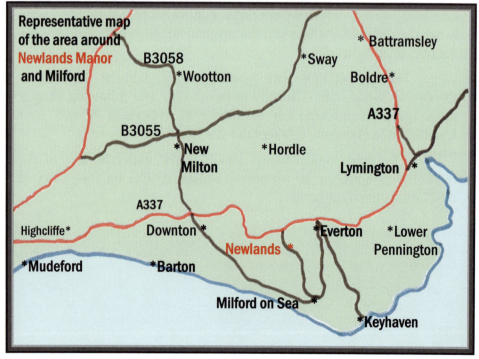

The Manor of Milford Montague, in which Newlands stood, dates back to Domesday, being one of three manors carrying the name of Milford. Specifically, Milford Montague was named as a result of a connection with the Montagu, Earl of Salisbury's family who owned the manor for some time. It then changed hands several times until it was owned by Admiral William Cornwallis.

The other two ancient manors, Milford Barnes and Milford Baddesley were later acquired by the Admiral and then Theresa Whitby after his death in 1819, and in due course they were to become part of the Cornwallis-West family holdings in that part of the country. It is also of interest to note that, as with many other coastal villages and towns around England, coastal erosion or other shifts have brought them much nearer to the shoreline. At Milford this process was exacerbated in the early 19th century so there would have been considerable changes to this coastline during the lifetimes of the people mentioned in this book. (This information is noted in *A History of the County of Hampshire: Volume 5* published in 1912.)

From the time when the Admiral first acquired the property, its history can be broadly divided into phases.

First, developments to improve the property and enlargement to a house of grand proportions; next, extension of the estate by acquisition of the adjacent manors; then, development of the pastoral and agricultural affairs of the property, followed by refurbishment of the house and grounds and further development of property towards the sea at Milford; finally the decline of the estate and its break up as a result of the impoverishment of the family and the bankruptcy of the heir.

The Admiral had earlier settled in Aldwick, not very far from Chichester and it was there he first developed his lifetime love of horses. Later, no doubt in order to provide more land for his country pursuits, he moved to Newlands. That property was not in very good order and had to be improved so, whilst Newlands was being made ready for his occupation, for a while William lived in what were no more than bungalow huts in the grounds.

However he had further aspirations and he continued to make

major changes to the property; especially during the period when he was 'resting' on shore between 1796 and 1801. This was the period after a court martial at which he had been acquitted but the Admiralty being churlish did not offer him any command.

The constructions he undertook in that period were quite considerable and they have culminated in the imposing structure which largely endures to this day. The architecture styled as Gothic, which is also known in an uncomplimentary way as 'Strawberry Hill Gothic', is ornate and splendid, as fine an example of that style as can be seen anywhere in Britain.

Credit for the works must however go to the ladies, as in the first instance with the Admiral being at sea from 1801 to 1805 after he set the works in hand, they all had to be overseen by a very talented and capable young lady, Theresa, the wife of Captain John Whitby. Her brother was to become a noted naval architect so it seems that the talent for design may have run in the family, as the subsequent generations carried on with a keen appreciation of, and a fine ability in artistic matters.

As will be noted in the following chapters it was after her husband and the Admiral died, that Theresa Whitby ventured into the production of silk by planting a thousand mulberry trees in the grounds. The activity within the Manor House and around the estate remained much the same whilst the Admiral and the Whitby ladies were in residence. Affairs were restrained and limited to comfortable country pursuits which the Admiral enjoyed. Theresa Whitby, on the death of the Admiral, continued in a similar vein. Later her daughter and Frederick West took over the estate, and although they lived in Florence for much their life, their way of living was very similar; certainly it was not over social. It was the later intrusion of the wild Irish blood of Patsy Fitzpatrick which brought about the revolution in lifestyle. Royal visits and parties then became the order of the day.

Theresa's grandson, William was the first person to be named Cornwallis-West, but he and his wife Patsy mainly lived at Ruthin Castle in North Wales whilst his mother was alive. However, in later years William spent time and money at Newlands in developing the additional land towards the sea which had been bought by his father

Frederick. These were new fashionable houses at the time, the results of which can be seen to this day.

The names of Whitby Road, Pless Road and Victoria Road remain in Milford as an indication of the family connection and the times in which the development was undertaken. The Agent at Ruthin, Dick Birch, spent a lot of time at Newlands on this development work, but it never really took off to the extent that the owners would have wished, and much of the funding was achieved by borrowing against the Ruthin estates. Parts of the developing estate were sold off in order to alleviate the strain on the family funds, but the money position was to remain very much under tension right up to the time of sale after the death of William in 1917.

In the meantime there were big changes made when Theresa Whitby's only daughter, Theresa West, died in 1886.

Patsy saw to it that quite a lot of the old furnishings were removed and the whole of the house was decorated more brightly. The gardens were re-designed and generally a great deal of money, which the family did not really have to spend, was lavished on Newlands. The property became a favourite for the rather elaborate parties of the Prince of Wales's set attending Cowes week, or at any other time for that matter. It also became a more convenient bolt-hole for Patsy and the Prince of Wales for any of their intimate relationships which were much rumoured at the time.

It seems that the remainder of the local populace may have been less enthusiastic towards the socialising lifestyle of the family, especially the ladies, in the Edwardian times - as when William died the local newspaper, *The Hampshire Chronicle* limited their remarks to 'He was well respected in north Wales'.

Some years before, when William had been concerned at the profligacy of his son George, he found a method to by-pass him from inheriting either Newlands or Ruthin, by arranging a permanent lease of both estates to the Prince of Pless, then his daughter Daisy's husband. However, the debtors would not have it; they petitioned the Courts and they won. Patsy had to leave, the bailiffs took possession, and that was the end of the Cornwallis-West family connection with Newlands. The furnishings and all that could be moved were sold and the lands of the estate were finally broken up. Surely the Admiral's and the two Theresa's bodies must have turned over in their graves at such a sad ending.

So for 120 years, from the acquisition by Admiral Sir William Cornwallis in 1798 until 1918, the house and manors were in his possession or that of his chosen beneficiaries, who became the Cornwallis-West family.

Newlands Manor in 1910
This would be in its hey-day before the rather restricted period of the Great War years and the relative impoverishment of the family.

Genealogy Cornwallis Family

The Cornwallis family has been extensive in its connections, so no attempt is being made to chart the full genealogy of the family. This simple version is to show some basic lines of descent and relationship.

Those who wish to learn more should refer to detailed reference sources.

Richard Earl of Cornwall (b 1209)
Walter le Cornwaleys (b 1232)
William le Cornwaleys (1300-1354)
Thomas Cornwallis (1335-1384); son John, settled at Brome, Suffolk, 1400
Thomas Cornwallis (son of John)
Thomas Cornwallis (b 1518) (knighted 1548)
Sir William – m Lady Jane (Bacon) (her 1st m) (2nd m to Sir Nicholas Bacon*)
  (*Culford Estate inherited in 1659 through this connection)
Sir Frederick (1st Baron Cornwallis of Eye 1661)*

Sir Charles (2nd Baron)

Sir Charles (3rd Baron) d 1698

Sir Charles (4th Baron) d 1722

	6th Son	7th Son
	Edward 1713-76	Frederick 1713-83
	General	Archbishop of Canterbury

Sir Charles (5th Baron)
(1st Earl)
d 1762 – m Elizabeth (eldest daughter of 2nd Viscount Townshend)

Sir Charles (6th Baron)	Harry	James (4th Earl)	**William**
1738-1805 (2nd Earl)	(d 1761)	1743-1824	1744-1819
(1st Marquis)		Bishop of Lichfield	**Admiral**
		and Coventry	

Sir Charles (7th Baron)
d1823 (3rd Earl)
         James (5th Earl)
(2nd Marquis)
         d 21.5.1852 (titles extinct)
(extinct)

(Culford estates sold 1823)

FOUNDATIONS OF THE CORNWALLIS-WEST FAMILY

THE ADMIRAL, SIR WILLIAM CORNWALLIS GCB
Picture by R Gardner in the private possession of and shown by courtesy of the 3rd Baron Cornwallis

CAPTAIN JOHN WHITBY   THERESA WHITBY
Pictures by J Hoppner on display at Sizergh Castle, Cumbria, owned and shown by courtesy of Henry Hornyold – Strickland Esq.

THERESA JOHN CORNWALLIS WEST (NÉE WHITBY)

THREE
THE ADMIRAL

Admiral Sir William Cornwallis was the youngest son of the 1st Earl Cornwallis, and brother of the 2nd Earl, General Charles. The latter became well known for his military career and administrative prowess, serving in America, India and Ireland, and he was further ennobled by being created the 1st Marquis Cornwallis. William was unmarried and remained so until his death in 1819.

The Cornwallis family had served the Crown loyally for several centuries. They had worked their way from the West Country to London and thence to a fine old estate in Suffolk near Bury St Edmunds. They gained another excellent estate nearby at Culford later by inheritance through marriage.

The family's origination in Cornwall is said to be from Richard, Earl of Cornwall; the surname Cornwaleys being used until 1335 with the birth of Thomas Cornwallis. It was his son John who moved the family to Suffolk into Brome Manor in 1400. A descendant also by name of Thomas, born in 1518, was knighted in 1548. A Sir William Cornwallis married a Jane Meautys but pre-deceased her; it was her second marriage as Dame Jane Cornwallis to Nathaniel

Bacon, son of Sir Nicholas Bacon, in 1614 which brought Culford into the Cornwallis family. The two daughters of this second marriage died in infancy and the one son, Nicholas, succumbed at an early age, shortly after completing his education. Thus, after her death, the whole of the Bacon and Cornwallis estates went to Frederick, Dame Jane's eldest son from her first marriage. In 1661 he was ennobled as the first Baron Cornwallis of Eye.

It was the 5th Baron, Sir Charles Cornwallis who became the 1st Earl in 1753. He had married Elizabeth, the eldest daughter of the 2nd Viscount Townshend, another very notable Suffolk family. Incidentally his twin brothers, Edward and Frederick, married two other daughters from the same Townshend family.

The union of Charles and Elizabeth then produced four sons: Charles, who became the 2nd Earl and later the 1st Marquis, Henry, James (who became the Bishop of Coventry and Lichfield) and William. There were also three daughters whose marriages created further links with other leading families in the land.

Thus William, born in 1744, was the youngest son of parents from two notable titled families in the county of Suffolk. It was a first class pedigree.

William attended school at Harrow for what seems to have been about two years before he was sent to join the Navy at the age of eleven, as was the custom to do so in those days. Starting as a boy sailor at that tender age, William then spent the next few years in learning the craft of being a naval officer, much of the time being involved in naval action in several locations.

His first ship was the *Newark* on which he went to America at the age of fourteen. He moved to the *Kingston,* taking part in the conflict at Louisburg. In 1759, having moved to the *Dunkirk,* he was back in England having taken part in defeating the French at Quiberon Bay off the coast of France near St Nazaire during the Seven Years War. He then went to the Mediterranean to fight the French again. By 1769 he was on the *Neptune,* the flagship of Admiral Saunders.

In April 1761 he was appointed acting Fourth Lieutenant of the *Thunderer*. Barely seventeen he had served on four ships, sailed several thousands of miles, fought in some campaigns and gained promotion. In addition, he later distinguished himself when in action against the French after an explosion and fire on his ship had caused much disarray.

In 1761, his brother Henry, known familiarly as Harry, died whilst serving in the army in Germany and in the next year his father died shortly before William arrived home to Culford on leave.

In those days the progress of young men through the ranks in the services initially depended upon being 'noticed', a process by which parents would see that their aspiring youngsters were drawn to the attention of higher ranks who could assist in their getting promotion. Elizabeth, as a widow, took over from her husband in making efforts on behalf of her youngest son, but letters show that she soon wrote to William telling him that he must make his own way by dint of his own talents and dedication to his work. It seems that William did just that, as the records for the next years indicate the progress he made within the senior service, and there are many references to his abilities.

In 1762 the young lieutenant was given command of a new sloop, the *Swift*, which was then under construction, and was sent to the West Indies, and he continued at this station until returning to England very early in 1765. During a short period at home, no doubt taking the chance to celebrate his coming-of-age, his first ambitions were achieved as a result of his qualities and his potential being recognised by the Admiralty. He was promoted to Post Captain.

He commissioned the *Prince Edward*, a twenty eight gun frigate in September of that year, but it was not until the following July that he sailed in the *Guadaloupe*, another twenty eight gun frigate, for the Mediterranean where one of his tasks was to be the protection of trade by British merchant ships. He had as much trouble from the merchant ships he was protecting, as from any aggressors. On at least two occasions he had the task of writing to the Admiralty to complain about behaviour towards Her Majesty's Officers and ships by those in the Merchant Service.

This young naval officer was now starting to show his mettle and this was to develop further in ensuing years. The British Navy was kept very busy at all times, with young commanders like William Cornwallis being very much at the centre of the action.

However, by 1769 he was back in England so that his ship could be fitted out in Plymouth for the West Indian station. In March 1770 he sailed for Jamaica and Haiti to gain as much knowledge as he could about the French dispositions.

William stayed on the West Indian station for the whole of the following year returning to England in June 1772. The *Gaudaloupe* was paid off in July of that year and he had some time on his hands. He took little interest in parliamentary matters as the MP for Eye (then in the gift of his family) and London social life was not to his taste.

In September 1774, he was appointed to command another sloop, the *Pallas*, which was heading for the West Indies, via the West African coast to search for pirates in the colonies, most notably for the prevention of slavery.

The Admiralty must have remained impressed with William's talents, as in January 1777 he was given command of a new ship of fifty guns, the *Isis*, together with three other sloops.

In April of that year, William set out with a convoy of transport vessels taking reinforcements to General Sir William Howe, the Commander in Chief of the British Army in America. The plan was to assist the army in the attack upon Philadelphia. He guided and guarded the ships carrying troops and stores up the Delaware Estuary and, after the collapse of Philadelphia, broke open the entrance of the Delaware. This campaign brought the young Captain Cornwallis to the attention of his naval superiors and confirmed him as a good sailor and a fine tactician.

William was first transferred to the *Bristol*, then to the *Chatham* at Rhode Island where he waited with other ships to convey back to England the shattered remains of General Burgoyne's army, which had surrendered at Saratoga to the rebel General Gates. They embarked in February 1778 and arrived in England by late March.

Once back, he saw to the fitting out of a new ship the *Medea* at

Bristol; by August he was given command of the *Lion*, an impressive 64 gun ship which was to serve him well in future conflicts. Owing to his popularity, most of his officers and crew asked to be transferred with him.

In 1779 he was again despatched to the West Indies and led an array of merchant ships in convoy that gave him as much trouble as his previous herd. He reported that 'much shot had to be wasted in firing cannon' to get some ships to remain on station in the convoy.

Later in the year news was received at home that the French had captured first St Vincent and then Grenada. A sharp engagement took place on July 6th when the French gave the British fleet under Admiral Byron a bad time, as Byron had ill prepared his ships for the battle. The *Lion*, one of the leading ships, was very badly damaged, so much so that Cornwallis had to take his ship off to Jamaica for repairs.

There, apart from meeting up with Nelson, an event which was to establish a friendship, William received many letters of concern for his safety and thanks for his safe delivery from serious harm. His superiors in London were very pleased with the way in which he had acquitted himself so well.

He was made Acting Commodore by March 1780. When the *Lion* had been repaired and was again fit for service, he sailed in the company of two other vessels which made a small squadron with 158 guns, a significant fighting force.

They were attacked by a larger French Squadron in the area of Mont Christi off St. Domingo led by La Motte Piquet, who felt that they could defeat the smaller British group. The British squadron gave more than its fair share in return, and the French fell away. The squadron set about chasing the French who rapidly withdrew. William was warmly commended for his fine initiative and determination in the face of a superior enemy.

Later near the Florida Gulf, a French fleet of seven ships of the line led by De Terney, with a force much larger than his own, challenged him. One of Cornwallis's ships, the *Ruby,* got into a most difficult position and was about to be cut off by the French. Cornwallis manoeuvred his small force to gather her back and shots were exchanged. Although he did not continue an engagement against so superior a force he had not hesitated to challenge it to save his colleagues. These incidents showed William's courage and his firm determination not to be deterred by superior odds.

Later in the year William was ordered back to England, taking with him Nelson who was in a poor state of health after the Nicaragua expedition. This cemented their friendship which was to continue for life.

In 1781 he was part of Admiral Darby's force sent to the relief of Gibraltar, but was back in England by May of that year. He was then given command of the *Canada*, which was regarded as being the very best ship in her class.

This appointment came with a letter extolling the merits of him being a very distinguished officer, most suitable for a ship of such excellence. By August they were sailing with Admiral Digby once more for the American coast.

During his last stay in those waters William on the *Canada* was part of a force which disembarked troops at Sandy Hook for the relief of his brother Charles at Yorktown; but the prevarications by the higher military command made this all too late. The soldiers were taken back on board and they sailed away again.

Subsequently William moved with his ship and the squadron to West Indian waters where more action awaited him.

The first of these was at St Kitts under Admiral Hood. The French fleet was twice the size of Hood's force, so Hood was inclined to stand away until he could be joined by Rodney. However, Admiral De Grasse, the French commander thought otherwise, that he would deal with the smaller force before any reinforcements arrived.

The battle which took place over two days in January 1782 showed the skill of the English Admiral in tactically beating the larger French fleet. The *Canada* was fully engaged and once again William distinguished himself in the action by frustrating the sailing way of the French Admiral's flagship in the engagement.

Two months later De Grasse and Rodney, with his enlarged fleet including Hood's ships, were to become fully engaged in battle, to be known as 'The Battle of the Saints', from its location by the Saints islands near Guadeloupe.

William in *Canada* again seemed to fulfil his own success in a robust way, and his abilities were well remarked upon. It is interesting that after the battle Rodney offered him command of the captured French ship *Ville de Paris* but the offer was declined; this proved to be a good decision as the vessel was lost by foundering during a storm in the Atlantic.

Letters between William and his brother Charles discussed the forthcoming appointment of Charles as the Governor General in India, the latter expressing the hope that William might be appointed as second in command to Admiral Parker in the East India station, but that was not to be so.

By the end of 1782 William was offered command of the *Foudroyant* lying at Plymouth, but this offer changed to the *Ganges*, which had become vacant, but then that was surpassed by his appointment to command the Royal Yacht.

The information about William Cornwallis for the next few years is somewhat thin on the ground at this less active appointment, and he settled down to a life of a gentleman.

Although he was the Member of Parliament for Eye, the gift of which lay with his brother the Earl, politics held little interest for him but pressure was put on him to stand for Portsmouth in the 1784 election by naval colleagues. He won the seat. Correspondence on the subject is sparse, and apparently the records of the House for the period give very little useful information. It can only be assumed William carried out his duties to the satisfaction of King George III and paid some attention to his task as an MP.

In 1787, William was appointed to command the *Robust*, and he received the honour from the King of being appointed as the Colonel of Marines at Plymouth. In 1788 he was appointed as Commodore and Commander in Chief of the East Indies Squadron.

An exchange of letters indicated that Nelson would have wished to forego his early delights as a husband in favour of action at sea, but all that William could do was to offer his friend the promise of a future vacancy. There is no indication that this caused any disruption to the friendship between the two of them.

In September 1789 Commodore William Cornwallis, flying his pennant on the *Crown*, reached Madras. He had been ordered to pay particular attention to the waters between the East coast of India and the Malayan peninsular, and to the Andaman Islands. The Dutch had a number of trading posts on the Malayan coast and were not anxious for the British to enter what they considered to be their domain. The Admiralty felt otherwise, and attached a surveying sloop, the *Ariel,* to the squadron for the specific purpose of surveying suitable harbour locations.

William then endeavoured to break the corrupt system of purchasing for ships stores and established the principle of receiving three tenders from potential suppliers, and for these to be considered without any inducements, which was received very favourably by the Admiralty. Whilst William held his command over the period of four years he was in East Indian waters, he kept a constant pressure on the matter. It is probably fair to say that this honest attitude did not find much favour with all his other naval colleagues and it certainly did not appeal to those in the supply departments who had been doing very well at the expense of the government and the sailors.

Nit-picking by the French over small incidents was indicative of the uneasy peace between the two countries. The strength of the French fleet in the East Indian waters of the Arabian Sea, Bay of Bengal and the adjacent parts of the Indian Ocean was not great by all accounts, yet they must have felt it necessary to magnify their importance, notably when neighbouring with the British in harbour, with whom they had been in conflict for so long.

William showed a considered courtesy in all his replies to any complaints. This being a measure of the man, who but a few years before had been in direct conflict with the French, that he should maintain a dignity commensurate with his office as Commander in Chief of His Majesty's Fleet in that area of the world.

William was an extremely fair commander who took the trouble to ensure that his officers in turn behaved with fairness to their sailors. Popularly known as 'Billy Blue', William was well known for enquiring about personal problems which might affect any of his men, officers or ratings, and he was held in the highest regard by all who served under him. In the course of his duty he was punctilious in ensuring that his officers did observe all the rules of etiquette amongst ships of various nations, and in seeing the correct courtesies being observed in harbour.

The talents of the two exceptional brothers, William and Charles, came together at a crucial time for Britain in its development of trade and consolidating its hold upon the Indian sub-continent. The first of the testing times was in the matter of Tipoo, Sultan of Mysore who in December 1789 attacked Travancore in Southern India.

It is worth considering just how this problem was dealt with by Commodore William Cornwallis at sea.

Right from the start William decided to be firm and made it his business to check and harass French ships. He was quite suspicious that the French were actually assisting Tipoo, and he took no chances. Instructions from London said that he was not to let any stores or other arms to be delivered to Mahé, or any other place on the Malabar Coast near to Tipoo's base, but to ensure that these were only allowed to be discharged at Pondicherry, the French port and enclave on the East coast. Whilst there was no need for direct intervention from the sea, it was necessary to retain naval presence, if only to deter the French should they try to support Tipoo.

Curiously, at the time when William was keeping an eye on the French, they were also receiving support from India to their garrison on Mauritius, which was in dire need of money and stores. At this time peace existed between the two countries.

It can not be said that Commander William Cornwallis was very heavily engaged in this Mysore war, other than this watching brief, although he was certainly kept in the picture by his brother and other contacts.

These worries did not prevent the Commodore from sailing

into the waters further to the East in order to carry out his duties in respect of establishing harbours in the Andamans, on Prince of Wales Island and on the Malay peninsular.

Having received instructions from Hood at the Admiralty in May 1791 to stop all French ships, William also pursued a policy of checking neutral ships.

The turn of the year 1791-92 brought the land war against Tipoo into its final stages, as General Charles Cornwallis moved to attack his last defensive fortress of Seringapatam. By February it was all over and Cornwallis on land was writing to Cornwallis at sea to give him the good news.

The year 1792 was one in which Commodore Cornwallis was to spend more time in his task of surveying the Bay of Bengal and the adjacent waters. He was assisted by his young friend and *protégé*, Lieutenant Whitby, in command of the *Dispatch,* who diligently sailed the waters of the bay, taking note of all suitable landfalls and other advantageous territories.

Prince of Wales Island, now known as Penang, which lay just off the Malayan coastline, had originally been annexed for the Crown by Sir Francis Light in 1786 on behalf of the East India Company, with an agreement from which the local Sultan of Kedah, who had it under his control, would benefit by financial payments in return for certain trading rights. By 1789 no payments had been paid nor had the treaty even been ratified by the Company and the Sultan was not a very happy man. William sailed to the island in 1791 to deal with the matter. It is interesting to record that Cornwallis issued instructions to all under his command to treat the natives on the various islands at which his ships docked with consideration.

These activities within the Bay of Bengal were taking place at the same time the fleet was involved in the stop and search policy against ships likely to be carrying arms to Tipoo. William had a wide ranging command, and he used it to the full.

Finally, the majority of the men-of-war were recalled home so he transferred his flag to the *Minerva* and was accompanied by the *Phoenix* as the only other battleship left with him. He was promoted to

Rear-Admiral of the White in 1792.

The declaration of war against France in February 1793 came just after the execution of Louis XVI but it was months before that news reached India, so it was July 1793 before Charles the new Marquis Cornwallis directed his attention to capture of the French enclave of Pondicherry.

William was not very safe as he now was commanding a solo ship, the *Phoenix* having been ordered home for repairs. He took over command of three of the East India company ships, and together with a privateer, the *Concorde,* which he had captured and refitted, formed himself an efficient force to block Pondicherry from the sea. The French surrendered on August 23rd.

After being relieved by Sir Peter Rainier, William sailed in the *Minerva* in October 1793, landing in England in late April 1794. On the way he stopped off at Diego Garcia, a remote island in the Indian Ocean which still remains a British territory of tactical significance.

On return to home waters William does not seem to have taken much of the leave granted to him, as within a very short time he was sailing with the Channel Fleet under Admiral Howe, but still flying his flag on the *Minerva*. Then by July 12th he had been promoted to Vice-Admiral (of the Blue) and moved to the *Caesar* a ship which he found quite unsatisfactory so he asked to be granted a change. This was to be to the *Prince* but even that was short lived as in December of that year he was given command of a brand new 100 gun ship, the *Royal Sovereign,* to which vessel he transferred with all his accompanying officers, including Captain Whitby with whom he had developed a long standing friendship.

By the start of 1795 William was in temporary command of the Channel Fleet. The routines he had to deal with were not of the most exciting: a minor mutiny on one ship and problems regarding the granting of leave to sailors which had been getting somewhat out of hand by requests not being made through the proper channels.

William by then had with him a small squadron of six ships including his *Royal Sovereign* and in June near Ushant, off the North-western tip of Brittany, they encountered a French convoy. Having chased away the escorting fighting ships they captured eight of the merchantmen.

A week later in the Bay of Biscay, Cornwallis and his ships met up with the French Brest Fleet commanded by Villaret-Joyeuse, an Admiral of considerable experience. The sequence of events which took place became known as 'Cornwallis's Retreat'; but there was nothing at all for him to be ashamed of as William's actions were greatly commended by all, with his naval skill and bravery being highly praised.

It was on the morning of June 16th 1795 when the British squadron sighted a 'substantial amount of sail' and within a short time the report came back that there were thirteen battleships, fourteen frigates and others, a far greater force than William's. He decided to withdraw but this was hampered by two of his slower vessels and the French gained on them, splitting forces in order to catch the British vessels between their two attacking arms.

William slowed down the retreat of his squadron in order to match the slower pace of these two ships and ordered the jettisoning of items to assist them to speed up. Nevertheless the French closed the gap and by nightfall they were in shot range and opened fire on the *Mars* which became damaged as a result, so that she was in danger of being cut off from the rest of her squadron. By this time William had raised the battle ensigns to make it quite plain to their enemy that they would fight, and so they did.

William set the *Royal Sovereign* on a course to cut between the *Mars* and the approaching French who had by now broken into three attack groups. He fired a heavy broadside at the French who swiftly fell back. For some extraordinary reason the ships under the French Admiral did not recover and press the attack, although they had the distinct power to do so. William was not impressed by this lack of determination on their part. The French sailed away, so by fighting back William's small squadron saw off the entire French Brest Fleet. This action was greatly praised by the Admiralty.

William was asked to accept the Order of the Bath from King George III but he declined on the basis that he had done nothing exceptional to merit the award. The event was marked in other ways by a 'Ballad of the Fleet', *Billy Blue*.

However, all was not to remain so pleasant for William; shortly afterwards there arose an occasion when the senior fleet commanders, including William, formed together to challenge a difficult instruction, and William took a strong position against the Admiralty.

When Marine forces were short, members of the army could be drafted on board to act in 'a like' capacity. Any ship's captain could have on board marines or soldiers, or perhaps even a mixture of the two. All personnel, from whatever source, were under command of the ship's captain. This was the cause of the trouble. The army did not like it.

Now as it was intended that many troops would be sent on board ships for a forthcoming expedition to the West Indies, it was felt by the Commander in Chief that all such disciplinary matters should be laid out in a precise form and an order was provided to the overall expedition commander.

These orders firmly established the naval commander as being pre-eminent on any ship, but that an immediate sentence could only be exercised *'with the agreement of the troops' commanding officer'*. The Admirals, on receiving knowledge of this very particular instruction, protested most strongly. William was outspoken and he added many strong words in bracing language to the Admiralty, which did not suit them. In the end a compromise was achieved which divided the discipline between the marines and other soldiers under command of the ship's captain.

William was later told that he was to be the Commander in Chief of the naval part of the West Indies expedition, and he sailed from England on 29th February 1796.

Scarcely had they left port when they encountered violent storms similar to those which had already caused the fleet to turn back on two occasions, resulting in a collision between his flagship, the *Royal Sovereign,* and a smaller transport vessel, the *Belisarius.* William went with his fleet to clear Finisterre, Northwest Spain, but then turned back with his flagship to Portsmouth to have repairs effected.

The Admiralty suggested that he should have continued with his journey on a frigate, the *Astrea*. William was not very pleased at this idea to travel in so ignominious a fashion without proper room for his staff, and he said so in letters to the Admiralty. He also made it clear that once the repairs to the *Royal Sovereign* were completed, he would sail forthwith.

William received a letter which intimated that it would be unwise to permit him to continue in command, followed shortly afterwards by one advising that he was to be subject to a court martial. Later in the same year, the case was heard by Lord Howe as President of the court, with senior officers, and William was acquitted of having refused a direct order.

William received many letters of congratulation, but he had to strike his flag under instruction from the Admiralty who by then had appointed another officer to the position. This put William on land from 1796 until early 1801 and it was during that time he moved his domestic interests to the South Coast, first at Aldwick near Chichester and later to Newlands at Milford in Hampshire, which features so much in the future events described in this book.

The year 1801 provided some government turmoil as Pitt had resigned as Prime Minister and another administration was formed. Earl St Vincent was appointed as the new First Lord of the Admiralty and on vacating the Channel Fleet by taking up his new office immediately offered it to William.

The announcement made mention of the very high regard of Admiral Cornwallis in the service as if he had not been resting on dry land for the previous five years. Congratulations came from many colleagues who welcomed him back at sea, including from his friend Nelson who had corresponded regularly with him during his recent enforced years of land life.

From here on, the events in which William was involved all led up to the Battle of Trafalgar. One of the major tasks was to be the blockading of the French Fleet, especially that in Brest, and in that task William Cornwallis was be the most successful commander of the campaign.

Later in 1801, as the French invasion fleet of boats gathered in Boulogne, it was felt necessary to try to reduce them to useless hulks, an enterprise taken on by Nelson himself, but it was not successful.

On October 1st a peace was agreed at Amiens and William returned to British waters, leaving only a few frigates on station to monitor the area, and he took himself to Torbay where his flagship *Ville de Paris* was sent for repairs.

Admiral St Vincent wrote to William later in that year to congratulate him on the success of the Brest blockade and the talents which he had brought to bear in successfully containing the French fleet.

The sailors were at an idle loose end and the first signs of unrest showed on the *Belleisle* but this was put down firmly by Captain Whitby. Later trouble broke out on a wider basis and this brought the sailors face to face with disciplinary action as some of them mutinied.

The Admiral called the ships' crews to order and reminded them of their duty and the consequences of insubordination, but some troublemakers continued with their dissent and there were scenes on various ships. Fortunately the junior officers, backed by the Marines who had remained loyal, quelled the troubles. By December 11th, eight days after the first mutterings of discontent had arisen, the mutineers were locked up. William then took the fleet to Spithead, tried the ringleaders and had them hanged by January 15th 1802, probably the most distasteful job in his whole naval career.

When the Treaty of Amiens was eventually signed on April 1st an order for demobilisation was issued and William left for his country retreat at Newlands where he rested from his exertions.

Peace with the French held until May 1803 when relations finally broke down. Immediately William volunteered his services to the Admiralty and on 10th May 1803 he was once again given command of the Channel Fleet.

Hostilities were declared on May 18th. William was given the *Victory* by the Admiralty on which to raise his flag and was ordered to sea to blockade Brest and generally to prevent the movement of enemy ships in the Channel. This task he undertook with remarkable efficiency which fully exercised his naval skills.

It was left entirely to William's discretion as to whether he retained *Victory* for his own purpose and as his flagship. William did not have to be asked and he just made over *Victory* to Nelson, who wrote to William with most grateful thanks.

Captain Whitby who had for years been William's closest confidant at sea and his official Flag Captain was by then serving with Nelson in command of the *Belleisle*. It is interesting to note that this young man was also held in equally high regard by Nelson. Although William asked for Whitby's return, the Admiralty did not comply with his request in the first instance.

William was extremely active in his task in defending the Channel. The Dutch were blockaded at Ferrol in Northwest Spain and all enemy small vessels, even fishing craft, were taken in charge and brought to English ports as the great fear of invasion by Napoleon was still very much in the air. 1803 was an extremely busy year for the Channel Fleet as it continued with the blockade at Brest, Cornwallis directing affairs from his station off Ushant.

Generally the British ships were kept busy, not only dealing with the French ships and their supporting shore batteries, notably at Brest, but also in keeping a clamp down on the many privateers in those waters. In respect of command William kept his staff fresh by moving them about, putting Collingwood first to Brest before bringing him to Ushant under him, and moving Pellew to Ferrol in lieu of Calder.

Towards the latter part of 1803 things became even more difficult for William as he had to diversify his Channel Fleet across a much wider area in order to take account of the possibility of a French invasion approach through Ireland and he sent part of his fleet to reinforce Admiral Gardner at Cork, and to create an independent squadron under Calder to watch the West Irish coast.

It had not been possible to release Captain Whitby, whom Cornwallis had asked to be sent to him as Flag Captain, until February 1804, but it was the end of June when he reported to Cornwallis.

Apart from an affair in planning to set fireships into Brest, which did not come about, the remainder of 1804 revived former scares that the French might still invade England across the Channel or via Ireland.

The winter weather was as bad as expected and the Admiral's own ship the *Ville de Paris* was damaged. Several of his other ships suffered in various ways and on many occasions they had to leave station for sheltered waters. However, the Admiral was one ever to be ready for action and the Blue Peter flag was kept hoisted so as to indicate to his fleet always to be ready to sail. It was this tradition throughout his long career which it is suggested led to him being nicknamed 'Billy Blue'.

Having endured the terrible winter, in March 1805 William applied for leave. He resumed his position of Commander in Chief on July 7th. By the time he got back on station the French fleet, apart from Messiessy and Villeneuve who had escaped, were very firmly locked up in Brest, Rochefort, Ferrol, and the Spanish at Cadiz.

William himself scoured a considerable area of ocean towards Finisterre trying to find Villeneuve and cut him off, but had no contact so he returned to the Brest area to continue the blockade. He became very frustrated by this lack of enemy contact and the chance of a good battle, and it showed in his tetchy behaviour, as reported by Captain Whitby.

Nelson, on joining up with William's fleet after his return from the West Indies, was ordered home and he immediately left to report to his superiors at the Admiralty. The friends did not actually meet on that occasion but Nelson wrote to him with presents of exotic foods from the West Indies.

William thought through his next tactical move whilst the Admiralty was still digesting the problem, and Nelson had scarcely left for England. On his own account he detached a considerable force of some twenty plus ships of the line under Calder to intercept

Villeneuve again off Ferrol. The Admiralty concurred with this decision. This large fleet of vessels subsequently formed the nucleus of the British fleet which Nelson commanded at Trafalgar.

The Admiral no doubt was aching to take on the main task of fighting the combined fleet but his first duty was to the blockade of Brest and the safety of the Channel.

Villeneuve, however, headed straight for the Mediterranean, so Napoleon's plan that the blockaded Brest fleet should break out and join Villeneuve to force the English Channel was stopped. One thing William achieved above all was that the Brest blockade continued to be held fast. This has been recognised as a considerable influence to the British fleet and greatly in Nelson's favour at Trafalgar, which was shortly to take place. Nelson did indeed owe William a considerable debt of gratitude in this regard, and some historians of Trafalgar have noted this.

It was only a matter of time before William heard that the battle at Trafalgar had taken place and that his friend Nelson had been killed whilst obtaining that notable victory.

Insofar as William was concerned he had not fought in any of the later major battles, and despite his bold effort to challenge the French fleets on more than one occasion, their reluctance to engage with him in any battle had frustrated him; but his contribution to the chain of events which led up to the ultimate conflict was remarkable.

However, he was treated very shabbily. The Admiralty did not even invite him to Nelson's funeral. It is also revealed by Whitby in his letters how much his Admiral was concerned and how he felt that political factions were working against him. Letters between William and his friend Lord Barham also disclose these concerns.

For Admiral Cornwallis events regarding his seagoing life moved to a fairly swift conclusion as in January 1806 Pitt died and the political map changed again. Charles Grey was appointed First Lord and this left St Vincent, out on a limb. He and William corresponded in a friendly fashion in which St Vincent was quite open in saying to him that he had offered his services to the Government.

Within two days of Grey finally being appointed as the First Lord he wrote to William advising him that St Vincent was to be given the appointment as Commander of the Channel Fleet. The opposition in Parliament, made a very strong complaint about what they perceived to be William's very unjust treatment, but to no avail.

Thus, on 22nd February 1806 at Torbay, Admiral of the Red, Sir William Cornwallis struck his flag for the last time and retired to his home at Newlands into a life of obscurity from his naval career.

In May 1814 he was made a Vice-Admiral of England but it was to be almost ten years after his retirement when he was honoured with the GCB in 1815, but by then he was not well enough to leave his home to be enrolled into the order. He died at Newlands in 1819.

Apart from John Leyland, who in 1899 compiled *Despatches and letters relating to the Blockade of Brest 1803-1805*, and who gave considerable credit to Admiral Cornwallis for his dedicated and skilful management of the Channel Fleet, his deeds had not been notably remarked upon until George Cornwallis-West wrote about his life and published several extracts from his letters in 1927.

Since then, apart from one section in a compilation of famous admirals of the time, his name has mainly been mentioned in places within other biographies or commentaries on naval actions. Some books published prior to the bicentenary of Trafalgar, which of course concentrated mainly on Nelson, did however start to give some credit to William Cornwallis for his considerable tactical ability and the way he helped to set up the trained fleet which was then to be so successful at the ultimate battle.

Whereas brother Charles received the plaudits of Parliament and the laudation of a grateful nation for his many years of service, with a substantial memorial in London, William remains unnoticed, except for the memorial in Milford Church which was erected by the daughter of his greatest friends, John and Theresa Whitby.

His retirement years at Newlands were noted for his interest in horses, parrots, support for the church and being charitable in the matter of the education of the young people in the parish. One of the two schools in the district was provided for forty young girls, and this was maintained by him.

On his death, as his nephew Charles, the third Marquis, had no heir at the time, the Admiral left his estate with the interest on the capital sum said to be £30,000, to the widowed Mrs Theresa Whitby, with a straight legacy of £10,000 to her young daughter Theresa. When Charles died in 1823, still with no heir, the capital sum passed to Mrs Whitby, much to the upset of both his and her families.

This short summary of the life of William Cornwallis is merely to set the scene for the consequences of this action in passing his property and name to the child of his constant friend Captain John Whitby and his wife Theresa.

THE WHITBY FAMILY CONNECTION

CRESWELL HALL, STAFFORDSHIRE
Birthplace of John Whitby
Courtesy of Staffordshire County Council

It will be useful to dwell briefly on the Whitby family and their home at Creswell, Staffordshire, although the only link with this story is through the one family member, John, who served with Admiral Cornwallis and their consequential friendship.

Whatever its earlier history, by the late 18th century Creswell Hall had been acquired by the Whitby family and it was to remain with them until well into the 19th century. Although the site of the Hall lies within the current parish of Seighford-with-Creswell, it was originally in an extra-parochial area, so the old parish records are amongst those of St Mary's, Stafford.

The parish register holds the date of birth of John Whitby as 7th October 1774, his father and mother being named as Thomas and Mabella, who had married at the same church on 1st February 1770.

Thomas Whitby would have been born in 1747 as he is recorded as having matriculated at Trinity College, Oxford on 18th January 1763 aged 16, later being created MA in 1768.

He was ordained as Deacon at St George, Bloomsbury, London, in 1779 and moved to be curate at Seighford in the same year. He was then ordained priest at Seighford and as vicar in 1780. He resigned in 1800, presumably in order to give way to his son Edward, whose details are given below.

The Reverend Thomas Whitby died on the 18th March 1828 having produced several children noted below:

John Whitby, his eldest son died on 6th April 1806, aged 32.

Edward Whitby was born in 1775 and died 23rd March 1852, having been Vicar of Seighford in 1800, adding Creswell in 1806, and his resignation is recorded in 1820, although he held the sinecure as Rector of Creswell from 1806 until his death.

Lucy Whitby, born on 29th March 1778, is shown as having married on 21st August 1798 Edward Berkeley Portman and giving birth to one daughter and two sons. One son, Edward, became the 1st Viscount Portman, the other son took Holy Orders.

George Whitby was born on 4th February 1780.

Henry Whitby, later Captain RN, was born on 21st July 1781 and died on 5th May 1812 aged 31, only one year younger than John.

Mary Whitby, born on 20th April 1786, married in June 1809.

In an ecclesiastical note about Edward, there is mention of a brother, Thomas. Clement is another name which has arisen, but to date no record of either of these has been found by the author.

It must have been shortly after the death of Edward, when Creswell Hall changed ownership into the Meakin family who were noted pottery manufacturers. It remained with them for some years, but changed hands at least twice before being damaged by fire in 1914, when the majority of the property was demolished, leaving only a few of the service buildings. It seems that these may subsequently have been incorporated into a newer property called 'The Mount'.

FOUR

CAPTAIN JOHN WHITBY

Although he was important in the lives of Admiral Sir William Cornwallis and Nelson, the records of this officer are more difficult to uncover. Those more readily available have enabled the following sketchy *résumé* to be completed. In this regard the author is grateful to Barry Jolly who has shared his findings of research.

John Whitby was born at Creswell Hall, Staffordshire on 7th October 1774 in the Parish of Seighford-with-Creswell and according to the register of Stafford St Mary held by Staffordshire Record Office was baptised on the same day. John was the eldest son of Thomas Whitby. His younger brother, Henry, also joined the Royal Navy.

References to John's birth in other places record his father as being the Reverend Thomas Whitby, but that would not be correct at the time as Thomas was not ordained until 1779, as recorded in the previous chapter. The register records him as being '*Esqr*'.

Little seems to be recorded of John's early naval career other than that he went to sea at the age of twelve and by April 1790 he had been gazetted as Lieutenant on the *Dispatch*. Unlike his later friend William Cornwallis, the author has not found a certain record of the vessels in which he served his time prior to that promotion.

John's period in the East Indian Station with Cornwallis was to be one where the latter came to rely on his ability. The young officer first came to the notice of Cornwallis when he was placed in command of the sloop *Dispatch*. John Whitby was active in the Bay of Bengal on that small vessel in surveying amongst the islands and acquiring interests for Britain.

On 20th April 1793 he was then promoted to be Captain on the *Minerva*, which became the flagship of Cornwallis.

Later, in 1794 he was appointed Flag Captain aboard the *Minerva,* and it was on this ship, commanded by John Whitby that Cornwallis sailed back to England at the end of his East Indies command, landing on 24th April 1794. This event is recorded in the log book of the *Minerva* by Captain Whitby, the last words being a reference to the fact that the then newly appointed Rear Admiral Cornwallis struck his flag.   *(See note on page 37)

It is interesting to note from George Cornwallis-West's biography, *Life and Letters of Admiral Cornwallis,* that he may have had a sense of foreboding about his trip home, as he is recorded as having made a will before sailing that if he should die at sea he should be buried as a simple sailor without any ceremony and that his possessions should be given to his friend John Whitby. So it can be seen that his much later bequest to Whitby's wife and daughter had a precedent and was not unusual.

During the period from 1796 until 1801 when Cornwallis was left by the Admiralty without a command, John Whitby continued his career as a Captain, at times sailing under Nelson's command, gaining considerable experience of his own accord.

In 1801 William Cornwallis was appointed Commander-in-Chief of the Channel Fleet. Other than a period of time from 1803 until June 1804 during which John Whitby served in command of *Belleisle* with Nelson in the Mediterranean, Cornwallis's contact with Captain Whitby was considerable.

In the meantime John Whitby married Theresa Symonds in 1802. Their first child, a girl Mary Anna Theresa died as a baby in 1803; the second, a girl who was named Theresa John Cornwallis, survived and is featured later in this story. There is some difference in the records of her date of birth, referred to later in this book.

War broke out with France in 1803 and Cornwallis tried to get Whitby back as his Flag Captain but it was not convenient at the time so Admiral St Vincent would not release him from his position with Nelson. The *Belleisle* seems to have been the last ship on which Captain John Whitby served in command under Nelson.

In his letter to Cornwallis of 4th February 1804 when Whitby was ordered to rejoin Cornwallis, Nelson adds a postscript, '*I can assure you I am not singular in regretting the loss of Whitby from our little squadron, it is universal.*' (Nelson –*The New Letters* edited by Colin White, page 31.)

However, on Whitby's eventual return to his appointment as Flag Captain with Cornwallis he was then to remain with him until the Battle of Trafalgar and thereafter until Cornwallis finally struck his flag and retired to Newlands.

It was during this period that the only reported intrusion of any disharmony between the two officers occurred. By then Whitby had considerable experience as a captain in his own right. By custom the position of Flag Captain, a sort of ADC for an Admiral, was normally that of a more junior officer trying to gain experience. Strains appeared in the relationship between the two, and they both wrote about this problem to Whitby's wife, Theresa, who was living at Newlands managing the estate. It was that capable young lady who came up with the solution which she presented to the Admiral in her letter to him in January 1806.

This is quoted by George Cornwallis-West in his biography of the Admiral. Theresa recommended to the Admiral that he should take a more junior Captain as his Flag Captain and then give the actual command of his ship, *Ville de Paris,* to her husband John. It is recorded that the Admiral took her advice and appointed a Captain Gosselin to the position of his staff officer as Flag Captain, John then taking command of another ship. Both William and John wrote effusively to Theresa commending her sound advice and good sense and their relationship reverted to its former happy state for the remainder of their time together at sea.

That was, however, not to be for long as new political masters decided on changes within a year after the Battle of Trafalgar (21st October 1805) and the Admiral was retired to shore.

There may be some dispute as to the facts of this happening in respect of the incident reference John's position as Flag Captain. A naval record shows that John was discharged from the *Ville de Paris* on 5th February and moved to command the *Gibraltar* from which he was discharged on 27th March 1806.

Captain Whitby was held in such very high regard by Nelson that it was he who was chosen to take the message of Nelson's death to his lover Lady Hamilton.

After Cornwallis's retirement in February 1806, John Whitby remained at sea in command, but that was not to be for any length of time as he was taken sick, although the nature of the specific debility is not disclosed. Whatever the illness was, it has been suggested that it was compounded by the pressure of continuous service at sea, not an uncommon malady in those times, even for the officers who had the benefit of superior accommodation and food.

It was to Newlands later in the same year that the very ill Captain Whitby was to return, and to die on 6th April 1806. It is from here that the story will shortly move on to a fresh chapter.

Before then it is worth noting that the life and naval service of Captain Whitby are not the most easy to ascertain. For a start there is some discrepancy concerning the matters relating to his age and appointments. The Naval Record Society gives his appointment as a Lieutenant to be 1780, but as the record of his birth and baptism at Stafford are shown to be 1774 that NRS record must be questioned.

It is stated that Whitby first went to sea at the age of 12, which from a 1774 date of birth would be in 1786, thus suggesting that his commission in 1790 would be at the age of 16. Now, at 16, this would be very young, but not totally unusual, as some young men with 'pull' had been appointed to a commission at that age, some even as young as 14. Then an appointment to Captain in 1793, and to that of Post

Captain in 1794, as recorded, would be remarkable, but not impossible.

It is commented throughout that Whitby had caught the eye of Cornwallis and Nelson as being extremely talented, so it would not be out of order for him to have achieved such a rapid promotion.

Further, records at the time of his death refer to his 'twenty years active service', i.e. from 1786 to 1806, and it was also noted in other places that when he died he was 'aged only 32'.

Everything therefore indicates that he was a very exceptional young man who made a name for himself with two of the most important and able naval commanders of the time, Cornwallis and Nelson. It is therefore all the more strange, indeed rather sad, that his naval career is so sparsely commented upon in other places.

Recent exchanges between the author and Barry Jolly suggest that there is the possibility some commentators may have become confused with another officer named Whitly. In any event, the author has decided that as this is a general piece and not a complete historical record, the information given above is sufficient to show the nature of the relationship between the various parties.

Author's note*. This log book from the *Minerva* came up for auction by Tennants of Leyburn in 2007. The author bid for it but was beaten by an enthusiast with a deeper pocket. The identity of the buyer was not disclosed.

Memorial to Admiral Sir William Cornwallis and Captain John Whitby
in the Parish Church of All Saints, Milford on Sea, Hants.

The above photograph of the memorial and transcription on the page opposite are reproduced here by kind permission of the Parish Church of All Saints, Milford, Provided to the author by Mr Alan Chapple of that parish.

In a vault at the western end of this churchyard are deposited the remains of the Honourable Sir William Cornwallis G.C.B. Admiral of the Red Squadron of His Majesty's fleet, Rear Admiral of England &c &c &c, son of James 5th Earl Cornwallis and brother of the first Marquis, by Elizabeth, daughter of the Marquis of Townsend. He was born February 20th 1744. As a naval Commander his services occupy a proud page in our national annals. He particularly distinguished himself in the command of the Canada under Sir George, afterwards Lord Rodney, April 12th 1782, in the West Indies. His celebrated retreat off Brest in which he withdrew his small squadron from an overpowering number of the enemy, on the 17th June 1795 was never equalled, and obtained for him the thanks of both Houses of Parliament. In 1806 he retired from the command of the Channel fleet to his seat, Newlands, in this parish, where he closed a well-spent life, after long suffering heroically borne, July 5th 1819, universally loved and respected. Practising every virtue, he was remarkable for truth, integrity, courage, benevolence, and unostentatious hospitality. In accordance with that modesty which was the distinguishing feature of his character, he left an expressed desire that no monument should be raised to his memory, which his successor Mrs Whitby, the widow of his friend and flag captain, deemed herself bound to obey, but this tribute to his virtues and the honour of his country, her daughter Mrs Frederick West feels it her duty to erect to the benefactor who cherished her infancy with parental solicitude, and whose memory she reveres with affection, gratitude, and admiration.

In the same vault with the ashes of his friend the Honourable Admiral Cornwallis who desired expressly to be buried beside him, are interred those of Captain John Whitby RN eldest son of the Revd Thomas Whitby of Creswell Hall, in the County of Stafford. He entered the Navy at the early age of 12 years, and during a period of 20 years was constantly and actively engaged in the service of his profession. Into the Minerva frigate, then bearing the flag of his patron, and friend, Admiral Cornwallis, he was made Post in 1793. He was brave and handsome, his heart tender, generous, and sincere. Zealous in his profession, loyal to his Sovereign, and attached to his country, he yet found leisure for cultivating vast and varied powers of mind with assiduous care, so that few subjects eluded his grasp. But it pleased providence to cut short a life of so much public, and private promise, and this gallant officer sunk under a brief but severe illness soon after his appointment to the Ville de Paris, on the 6th April 1806, at Newlands, in the County of Hants. Deeply and deservedly lamented.

In the same vault reposes the body of Mary Anne Theresa Whitby, daughter of the late Captain Thomas Symonds and of Elizabeth Malet his wife who was born December 18th AD 1784 and rendered up her soul to God August 5th 1850 suddenly, and painlessly, at Newlands in this parish. The affectionate and faithful wife of John Whitby Esq Post Captain Royal Navy, she possessed unfeigned piety, and masculine sense, with every feminine charm of person. the desire of being useful to her species, and cordiality towards numerous friends who lament her loss. Her intellect was penetrating, her accomplishments varied, she was the benefactress of the poor, and the stay of many. Her grateful and afflicted daughter raises this memorial to an excellent mother, tenderly wept, and affectionately beloved, trusting in the hope of a blessed resurrection, and reunion in the kingdom of heaven.

Also to the memory of Theresa J Cornwallis West, of Newlands Manor in this parish, widow of Frederick R West of Ruthin Castle, North Wales, born May 1st 1804, died September 18th 1886. My purposes are ended, and the thoughts of my heart: but my trust is in thee, my God and my Redeemer. Have mercy upon thy servant O Lord, and blot out all my transgressions.

FIVE

THE MOTHER

Mary Anne Theresa Symonds, John Whitby's wife, was born on 18th December 1784. She was the daughter of another naval officer, Captain Thomas Symonds, who was a very old friend of William Cornwallis from their earlier shipmate days.

The same Thomas had been associated with William's older brother, the 2nd Earl, when he had been the officer in charge, on the *Guadaloupe*, of the small squadron of ships at Yorktown which had assisted in its defence against the French from the seaward side. Thomas Symonds joined with Lord Charles Cornwallis in signing the final documents of capitulation at Yorktown.

One of Theresa's brothers, William who also joined the Navy, was knighted and became a Rear-Admiral and was a well-noted naval architect. Another brother, Thomas, became an Admiral; his son, Captain W. Cornwallis Symonds, died somewhat young whilst serving in Antipodean waters in 1841. Plainly the name Cornwallis meant much to the Symonds family. Theresa was only nineteen when she married John Whitby.

Information about Theresa's family background indicates she was very 'well connected', coming from a notable Suffolk family of an extensive nature which was also to become well known in the Milford area. One of her sisters, Sophia, later married William Reynolds and they lived close to Newlands Manor, at Milford House, which was on part of the enlarging Cornwallis estate.

It seems from the record, as described by George Cornwallis-West in his *Life and Letters of Admiral Cornwallis,* that the young couple must have lived with the Admiral at Newlands for most, if not all of their married lives. Theresa was left with a brief to manage most of the estate affairs, including a considerable development of the house, whilst her husband and the Admiral were at sea. In fact the Admiral made over to her the powers of attorney so that she could act on his behalf in legal matters as was necessary to manage his affairs.

To give this considerable duty, indeed a burden, to such a young woman speaks considerably of the faith he must have had in her ability. We know that she was fluent in three foreign languages so her education must have been good, and her talents exceptional. In the light of her consequent business approach to various affairs after the death of the Admiral she must have been as remarkable as was her husband, John Whitby.

When John Whitby died in 1806, his daughter, who was also called Theresa, was barely a year old. Theresa, his widow, was only twenty three.

On the death of her husband Mrs Theresa Whitby moved away to live with her sister Juliana at her home in Fareham and the retired Admiral William was then destined to live alone. His interests were with his horses, parrots and the time he took in developing local educational activities, and the church to which he was a devout adherent.

It was about a year later when Mrs Whitby, accompanied by her daughter and her sister, returned to live at Newlands but this arrangement did not last long, as her sister left to get married. This time Theresa was destined to live on her own with her daughter as all her other sisters were also married.

However, she and the Admiral were both lonely and when he wrote to her suggesting that 'as his daughter' it would be doing both of them a favour, she went back to live at Newlands. George Cornwallis-West in his biography quotes from the letter which he wrote to Mrs Whitby:

'God knows best, my dear Theresa, what arrangements you will make. I will only say (what I trust is wholly unnecessary) that at all times I shall be glad to see you here. Can you not bring yourself to solace the remaining years of an old man, who has ever looked on you as his daughter, and who has flattered himself that his affection and regard were in some means returned.'

Plainly moved by this heartfelt appeal for her company, the equally lonely Theresa Whitby quickly returned to Newlands with her daughter.

This theme of regarding her as his daughter was one which had characterised their relationship. Mrs Whitby's own father had died when she was very young, so no doubt there could have been a substitute parent factor there.'

The correspondence referred to by George Cornwallis-West showed that his family was quite delighted at this arrangement, especially his brother James, who was the Bishop of Lichfield and Coventry. Theresa Whitby and her daughter then lived at Newlands for some twelve years until the Admiral died on July 15th 1819. Then, as the estate was bequeathed to Mrs Whitby and her daughter in trust, they continued to live there.

Curiously, despite the two families being quite happy with the domiciliary arrangement at the time, when the Admiral had died they turned against Mrs Whitby only, it appears, with the exception of the Admiral's nephew, the 2nd Marquis Cornwallis and the Bishop, both of whom continued to correspond with her.

George Cornwallis-West remarks that Mrs Whitby's family were more upset than the Admiral's. It may well be that the terms of the will created this antagonism. Apart from a few special legacies, all the estate was left to Mrs Whitby and her daughter and then in further trust for any son of her daughter, Theresa.

It had originally been written into William's will that the five daughters of Charles, his nephew, would receive an interest if he had a son and heir. However, Charles died in 1823 without an heir, so his daughters received nothing. These were reasonable grounds for them to feel piqued and to add to their loss, their father had been less than careful in his management of the Brome and Culford Estates which were subsequently sold off. The Marquisate died out, but the Earldom transferred back a generation to Admiral William Cornwallis's other surviving brother, James, Bishop of Coventry and Lichfield.

Theresa, who was only thirteen, was present holding William Cornwallis's hand when he died. The impression on the young girl was considerable and when she was older she had a memorial raised in Milford Church. This was in conflict with the Admiral's wishes that there be no memorials and that he only should be buried alongside his friend John Whitby. Mrs Whitby adhered to that request but her daughter did not.

Mrs Whitby and her daughter Theresa carried on living at Newlands Manor and they both developed very strong links with the local community, which continued until Theresa's death in 1886.

Mrs Whitby pursued her artistic and creative interests, one being the rearing of silkworms to making silk, an activity she continued until her death in 1850, attaining a high degree of recognition for her work in this.

The estate at Newlands was reportedly planted with a thousand mulberry trees, which had been imported from Italy in April 1836, and the silk itself was woven in nearby Milford as a cottage industry. Mrs Whitby was so determined to make the business a success that she imported a French silk winder to train her own girls in the proper method of winding the silk. By 1844 the first good quality silk was produced. Products from this enterprise were in steady demand and, Eileen Quelch, biographer of George Cornwallis-West, in her book *Perfect Darling* mentions that a gift of *'twenty yards of crimson and gold damask'* was made to Queen Victoria in 1848.

At least one Manchester manufacturer, a Mr Louis Schwabe, purchased large quantities for commercial use.

Mrs Theresa Whitby also wrote a manual on the rearing of silkworms in England, published in 1848. There are records of her exchange of correspondence on the subject with Charles Darwin and she later received recognition from the Royal Agricultural Society of England for her continued and determined efforts in this unusual, for England, textile manufacture.

An interesting article on this aspect of Newlands Manor life was written by Angela Harris and published in the Milford-on-Sea Record Society Occasional Magazine in April 1917:

'Mrs Whitby, following the Admiral's death, in her ensuing life at Newlands Manor had continued to run the house in the way it had been the custom under the Admiral, with little or no changes to its style or decoration. Her daughter was in due course to follow in her footsteps after her death, but in the remaining years of her life until she died in 1850 Theresa Whitby carried on exercising her skills in fine crafts. She is recorded as a landowner, antiquary and artist and the business she set up as a producer of silkworms and silk weaving. Sadly, despite the work she had put into the latter, when she died the production of silk and the whole business died with her.'

In addition to those business interests she continued to show the same care for the community as had the Admiral. One of these interests was in education and it is recorded that she provided the funds to pay for a school building completed in 1841 which survived until 1968. The commemoration stone still survives, having been incorporated into a residential building on the same site. It is scarcely surprising that Theresa showed this interest as, after all, her own education had obviously been of the highest standard.

However, it is interesting to note that Theresa was partial to the support of the girls in educational matters as it is recorded that she only gave one guinea to the boy's school founded in 1818, (the Bishop of Winchester gave three guineas) whereas her generosity to the girl's school and a national Sunday school were the recipients of much more, as had been the custom of the Admiral.

Furthermore, that culture of Theresa Whitby and her talent in art and crafts, as well as her charitable efforts, lived on through her child, grandson and her great grand children. Of the latter, Daisy was to set up a profitable lace making business and she encouraged that neglected industry of Silesia in Germany so that it should provide work for the unemployed of the district in the rather bleak years preceding the First World War.

Mrs Whitby acquired further property interests in the area after the death of the Admiral, and she managed these interests with the same care she had shown when left to do so by the Admiral in her younger days. Whilst the Admiral was still alive she purchased the Manors of Milford Barnes and Milford Montague, and shortly after his death acquired that of Milford Baddesley. By the 1840s she was holder to the title of about 30% of Milford, and in addition she had increased the Newlands estate to about 200 acres. However, in her mature years, although continuing to be extremely generous to local charities, it is remarked that perhaps she had become a somewhat domineering figure in the locality.

Theresa, Mrs Whitby's only surviving daughter, was to meet and marry Frederick Richard Myddleton West, a grandson of the 2nd Earl De La Warr in September 1827. Although this marriage was the second for Frederick, whose first wife had died, it may have been partly coincidental that the Countess De La Warr was an old friend of the Admiral. She had helped and comforted Theresa's mother, Mrs Whitby, after the death of her first child when her husband John and the Admiral were both away at sea, a fact which is clearly recorded in the biography of the Admiral.

Whilst Mrs Whitby was alive, her daughter and husband did not spend much time at Newlands, either living at Arnewood nearby or much preferring Ruthin Castle, the season in London, or living in Italy.

Mrs Whitby, her daughter Theresa and her husband Frederick West all had an artistic nature and the young couple spent much of their early married life together in Florence, a haven for so many cultured English people. Their son William was born there in 1835. He would in due course be known as William Cornwallis-West and this was truly the start of a new family name.

We must now look at the circumstances which bring the historical West family name into a link with that of the Admiral. He had come from a lineage of considerable distinction, but the ongoing link which he then created was to be one by paper inheritance alone, not by blood line. So, our story now progresses to another generation.

But for Mary Anne Theresa Whitby it is simply necessary to record that she died at Newlands quite suddenly, aged 66 in 1850 of no identified ailment.

THE DE LA WARR (WEST) GENEALOGY

This simple chart is merely to disclose some basic historical links. Any readers who wish to find out more detail should refer to appropriate records.

Note. The family name of De La Warr changed to West within the life of Reginald, 6th Baron, 1394-1451.

Roger De La Warr 1320 1st Baron of 1st Creation in 1299
ad sequitor to
William West 1520-1595 1st Baron of 2nd Creation in 1572
ad sequitor to
John West 1st Earl De La Warr 7th Baron of 2nd Creation
   1693- 1766 |
John West 2nd Earl De La Warr – m 1756 Mary Wynyard
   1729-1771 | d 1784
1. William West. 3rd Earl De La Warr 1757-1783
2. Hon Frederick West –m (2) 1798 Maria Myddleton (of Chirk)
   1767- 1852 | d 1843
Frederick Richard West married 11.9.1827 Theresa John Cornwallis Whitby
     1799-1862   1805-1886

1. Frederick Arthur Myddleton West b 29.7.1828 d 21.11.1828
2. Frederick Myddleton West b 31.8.1830 d 13.8.1868
3. Georgiana Theresa Ella West b 28.12.1831 d 8.2.1915
4. Florence West b 2.11.1833
5. **William Cornwallis Cornwallis-West** b 20.3.1835 d.7.1917
6. Theresa L S E West b. 9.8.1839 d 4.10.1920**
** This information taken from a memorial tablet in Milford Church
   Note: Debrett's mentions a Daughter born 9.11.1839

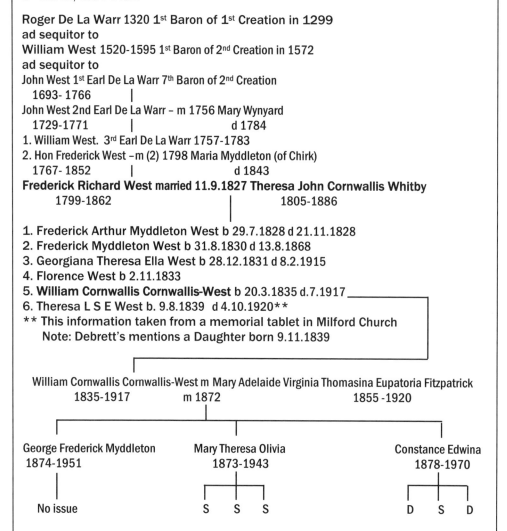

William Cornwallis Cornwallis-West m Mary Adelaide Virginia Thomasina Eupatoria Fitzpatrick
     1835-1917   m 1872   1855 -1920

George Frederick Myddleton	Mary Theresa Olivia	Constance Edwina
1874-1951	1873-1943	1878-1970
No issue	S S S	D S D

For further issue refer to 'The Next generations' genealogy on page 144

SIX
DEVELOPMENT
OF
THE FAMILY
THE RUTHIN CONNECTION

Ruthin Castle, in Denbighshire, North Wales was originally built for King Edward I who then, in 1277, gave it to Prince Dafydd ap Gruffydd. However, that was not the first castle on the site above the Clwyd valley as there seems to have been a lesser structure in that location from much earlier times.

Within a few years the castle had changed ownership and the new incumbent, Reginald de Grey, made significant improvements in 1282 and even more grand developments in 1295. The development of these works is described in detail in *The History of Ruthin Castle* by Reginald de Hereford.

In 1400 the castle was stormed by Owen Glyndwr, but not successfully; it then changed ownership to Henry VII, reputedly as payment of a gambling debt, and remained loyal to the Crown in the Civil War.

The much later connection with the Cornwallis-West family came about in a somewhat circuitous way.

The Myddleton family who lived nearby at Chirk acquired it at the Restoration. They were a local family who were cousins to the West, De La Warr, family. It was then in 1798 that Frederick, the younger son of the 2nd Earl De La Warr, took as his second wife Maria, the daughter of Sir Richard Myddleton, and they had a son, Frederick Richard West.

The family Myddleton had by then in their care properties at

Chirk and Ruthin Castles, and a number of lesser establishments in the district and wider country within North Wales. Although their main residence was at Chirk Castle, where everyone seemed to live, all was not harmonious especially between the two brothers-in-law who were the husbands of the two married sisters, Maria and Charlotte.

Indeed it was quite the opposite, especially in the matter of the division of the properties, and a great deal of money was spent in fighting their various corners and claims. In the end, the case went to Chancery and the House of Lords. After spending all that money, the decision was still not to their liking so the family drew lots, supervised by the local schoolmistress, to decide just who would have what. Eventually, although Maria took a property at Llanarmon, Frederick's family was to benefit in the end as the sister Harriet, who had not married, inherited Ruthin Castle, and then passed it on to her nephew, the young Frederick Richard West.

This nephew married Theresa Whitby, the daughter of John and Theresa Whitby, after his first marriage ended with the death of his young wife. It was Frederick and Theresa's son, William, who was to become the first Cornwallis-West and in due course the owner of Ruthin Castle.

In 1826 a house was built on the site within the two baileys which had formed the original and modified castle structure, a house which the young Frederick Richard was to develop even further by some rebuilding and extensions in the period from 1849 to 1852.

In order to fund the refurbishment Frederick had mortgaged the property, so it was just as well that he married Theresa, an heiress of some substance in her own right, as the sole beneficiary of the estate of Admiral Cornwallis GCB.

Later, William's wife, Mary, or Patsy as she was then widely known, would beautify the grounds with different planting projects although William's parents had done much already to improve the artistic amenities of the estate with the statuary they had brought from Florence.

When the Lord of the Manor, William Cornwallis-West died in 1917 the Castle had to be sold to meet the debts of creditors. At first

Ruthin became a hospital, but in later years it changed into a hotel of some quality, and that is how it remains to this day.

RUTHIN CASTLE SHOWING PART OF THE 19th CENTURY BUILDING TOGETHER WITH THE MOAT AND PARTS OF THE ORIGINAL CASTLE
Published here by kind permission of Anthony Saint Claire,
Chairman of Countrypark Hotels Ltd

SEVEN

THE DAUGHTER

Theresa John Cornwallis Whitby, the daughter of John and Theresa Whitby was born in 1805. There is confusion as to the actual date of her birth as on one memorial in Milford Parish Church it is shown as 1st May 1804, whilst on another as 1st May 1806. It is said in certain notes that she was born about eighteen months after the birth and death of a first daughter in 1803. Therefore 1804 seems unlikely, so 1805/1806 is probably the best assessment. Of these dates, 1805 is quoted in several places, including in Diana Coldicott's history of Milford House, so that seems to be most likely year of her birth.

The matter can, however, be settled by reference to the Parish Register of the Milford church which records that she was baptised on May 4th 1805 by Samuel Smith, Curate, and she was received into church on June 9th 1806. As baptisms in those days took place within days, often merely hours after the birth, it seems highly unlikely that the birth would have been much before the date of the baptism in May 1805. One can see how the error on one memorial could arise due to the 1806 date noted above, but how that of 1804 occurred is quite a mystery.

Little is recorded of her childhood years, although after the sudden death of her father in 1806 they would have been somewhat peripatetic. She was moved first from Newlands Manor in Hampshire to her aunt's home for one year, then back to Newlands for another year, away again for a period, then after the Admiral's appeal to her mother, returning finally to Newlands where she lived until she married in September 1827 at the age of 22.

It is not recorded how the young Theresa met her husband to be, Frederick Richard West. It may be that his grandmother who had been a friend of Admiral Sir William Cornwallis and who had helped Mrs Theresa Whitby after her first child died soon after birth had kept in touch with her, and that the meeting came about that way. Frederick had already been married to Lady Elisabeth Stanhope who then died in childbirth, so this well may have been the case that the two were drawn together by the machinations of older ladies.

After their marriage, Theresa and Frederick lived abroad in Florence for several years where some of their children were born. They both had a keen interest in art, a talent prevalent on her mother's side. Their life in Florence plainly influenced William, one of their sons, of whom more will be said later.

When her mother died in 1850, Theresa West took over the care of Newlands Manor and saw to it that the house was kept in the way it had been for the Admiral, until her death in 1886. Her husband died in 1868; thereafter she lived a somewhat reclusive life, but she took great interest in local educational work. This was something which had also been one of the Admiral's charities. In addition she had a talent for writing stories and she maintained good contact with some other writers of the times.

Active state interest in education only commenced in 1833, but concerns began to be expressed in various reports emanating as early as the late 18th century. Prior to 1833, education for the poor was almost entirely provided for by charity.

In respect of education, the Admiral had originally endowed a school for forty young girls which had been recorded in an otherwise uncomplimentary 1818 Parliamentary report on the state of education in the Milford Area, where there was only one other small school.

The situation in Milford was described in the Report as: '*Two schools on the National plan – one supported by voluntary contributions amounting to £40 p.a. and having 27 scholars; the other maintained by Admiral Cornwallis consisting of 40 girls who are clothed.*'

Theresa's mother, Mrs Whitby, had carried on in the same spirit as the Admiral and in 1841 paid for a school to be built on the High Street and this survived in one form or another until 1968 when it was demolished, although the name stone is retained in the garden wall of a property on the site.

Later, in 1851, it was Theresa West who donated a plot of land on Lymington Road for the building of a new school which was completed in 1852. In 1856 the two schools, the one from 1841 and the new one were run together and the copy of the Rules which is depicted in this book survives as part of that time. Theresa continued to donate generously for its maintenance and improvement until her later years around the 1880s.

There were some problems regarding the school's funding as Mrs Whitby's will had been rather specific in its clauses, but after Theresa West's death in 1887 these were resolved and the fund was able to be satisfactorily wound up in due course.

This philanthropy was continued in some way by her son William; as late as 1897, despite not being over rich due to poor revenues from attempts to develop the estate, he donated land to improve the school's sanitary facilities when it had to be temporarily closed because of serious concerns in this regard.

However, this very short treatise on the educational facilities in Milford shows how Theresa West carried on from the examples set by the Admiral and her mother in endeavouring to bring education to the working people of the district.

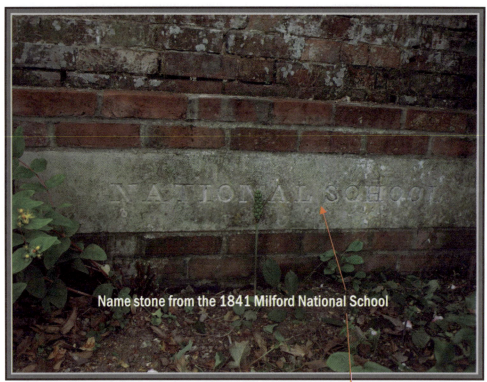

Name stone from the 1841 Milford National School

Milford National School 1841 – 1856
'Belmont', 114 High Street, was built on the site, extended in 2002 and re-named 'Riverside'.

Picture of the 1841 school
Courtesy of Mr Bob Braid of the Milford-on-Sea Historical Record Society

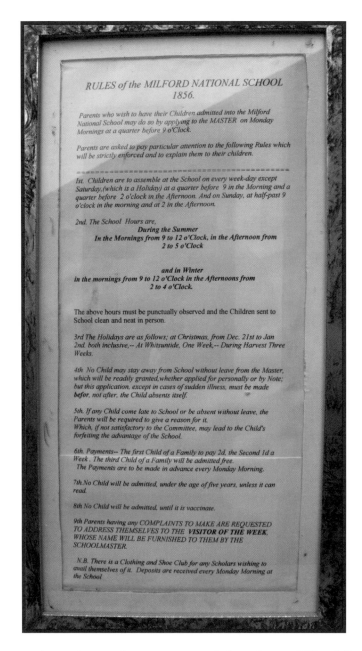

The copy of a notice setting out some of the rules at Milford National School in 1856, together with the picture of the school name stone from the 1841 school, shown opposite.
Courtesy of Jacci Rhodes-Jury of the house Riverside which is built on the site of the 1841 school, where the stone is built in to the garden wall.

As the owner of Newlands Theresa set about the task of raising a memorial in Milford Church to Admiral Cornwallis, for whom she had plainly retained a great affection. This, of course, was against the Admiral's strict wishes, to which her mother had rigidly adhered, but in hindsight it is good for posterity that Admiral Cornwallis's last resting place is properly recorded. But for that, in view of the absence of any other national memorial to commemorate his years of loyal service to his country, the Admiral would remain largely unnoticed.

However, in accordance with his other wish to be interred alongside the body of his old friend and shipmate, John Whitby, the memorial in the church, which is shown at the end of this chapter, records their service and friendship.

A lady of strong principles, Theresa was not at all inclined to the frivolities which were becoming the fashion amongst the younger royals and their adherents. Although her earlier married years when they lived in Florence must have been happy and gay, on the death of her husband she tended to adopt a more quiet and austere lifestyle. Visitors to Newlands were mainly limited to those whom she wished to see for friendship, not for their position or other social niceties.

Her mother, as previously noted, had added to the Newlands estate during her lifetime and whilst her husband had been alive he had added to the estate locally including the purchase of additional land at Milford-on-Sea and he had acquired some more land around Ruthin in Wales. As a result, his widow Theresa was well catered for and she lived out her years in financial comfort. Theresa's first born son died at birth, she had another son who died before she did and three daughters, two of whom married and one remained single, but this book will only relate the succession of events regarding the surviving son, William, in the next chapter.

The relationship between William's mother and his teenage wife was fairly strained from the outset. Theresa felt that the young lady in question was not the right one for her son, as she was involved in the rather fast Prince of Wales set and came from an Irish family which was then considered to be rather dubious in reputation, at least on the female side.

Theresa was not at all impressed with the proposed nuptial arrangement. The Cornwallis family, under whose wing she had been raised, had given generations, indeed centuries of service, to the Crown. Their reputation for almost straight-laced courtesy and good behaviour was well known. The frivolities of Edward Prince of Wales and his entourage were of no interest to her. The thought of a wild seventeen-year-old daughter of an already scandalised mother who was beginning to acquire her own reputation, marrying her son was not one for which she had any sympathy. She set her mind against the marriage, and did all she could to persuade her son that he was being taken for a ride to suit the convenience of the Prince and his lover Patsy Fitzpatrick.

However, William, Patsy and the Prince prevailed and so the wedding took place. Theresa did not attend.

Some months later when a first child was on its way, Theresa seemed to have a change of heart and made a great effort then by organising a magnificent ball at Newlands. It was not to be a success at repairing the relationship as young Patsy behaved badly.

That was it as far as Theresa was concerned; she banned William's wife from Newlands for life and Theresa never spoke to her again. William remained in her affections, but it was not to be until after Theresa's death in 1886 that Patsy was able to get her hands on Newlands, when she changed the old fashioned decorations and style to the lighter touches of the later Victorian and Edwardian eras.

Previously they had lived at Ruthin and in their London house. By the time she was twenty-one Patsy had not only given birth to the daughter mentioned above, but also a son and another daughter. The children were named Mary, George, and Constance respectively but the two girls were widely known by their pet family names of Daisy and Shelagh for the rest of their lives. George had a family nickname, Bussie or Bassie, but he remained as George in the wider circle of public knowledge.

Grandmother Theresa, who was by then living on her own at Newlands, was put into the imagination of the young children by their mother Patsy as a sort of ogre, but on one visit by George to Newlands he recalls being cared for almost to the point of obsession. In his book *Edwardian Hey-Days* he says:

> 'As, however, I was the heir, Grandmama West so far relented as to have me stay with her and one of the aunts when I was boy of twelve. A large dinner-party was given, to which all the neighbours were invited and at which I formed the principal exhibit. Every mouthful I ate was carefully watched, to see that I did not over-eat myself, and when the meal was over I was solemnly placed at a table and told to play draughts with a young lady guest, while the rest of the party looked on. It was one of the most awful moments of my life, and of the young lady's too, I imagine. The next morning I expressed a desire to go and fish in the lake, and after a great deal of demur, my grandmother consented, but was so terrified lest I should be drowned that she insisted on her butler accompanying me, and stipulated that a cord should be tied around my waist, the end of which should be firmly fastened to a tree!'

George was the only one of her grandchildren by William and Patsy that Theresa West ever saw at Newlands, the girls did not go there until after she died.

As a postscript, some comments about the future generation disclose that Patsy and her daughter Daisy were both to have a fairly significant involvement in political affairs during their lives, one in England, the other in Germany. George and Shelagh were to lead less public existences. William himself, after putting aside any of the frivolities of his youth and formative years in the artistic community of Florence, including it is recorded three illegitimate daughters, was to buckle down to being a pillar of county society.

It is from this point that we now look at the individuals who made up the Cornwallis-West family, which in name spanned from William's birth in 1835 until 1951, when the last of that name died.

Thereafter any blood line continuation was to be under different family names most notably that of the Prince of Pless, but also through the female line of Shelagh's marriage to the 2nd Duke of Westminster.

George, who married three times, had no children, so there is no direct Cornwallis-West male bloodline.

A footnote to this short chapter on the young lady who, as it were, founded the Cornwallis-West family is shown on the memorial tablet in Milford Church. It was organised by her daughter, Theresa Lucy Sophia Elphinston West, who survived all her siblings, dying in 1920.

Memorial to Theresa John Cornwallis-West*

Taken by Alan Chapple and reproduced here by kind permission of the parish.
*It was her son William who changed the name to Cornwallis-West in 1886, the year his mother died

THE WILD WEST SHOW

WILLIAM
CORNWALLIS – WEST

MARY (PATSY)
CORNWALLIS – WEST

Pictures (artist unknown) in the possession of
Countrypark Hotels at Ruthin Castle Hotel
shown here by kind permission of Anthony Saint Claire, Chairman.

GEORGE

© The National Portrait Gallery, London

DAISY

Courtesy of Muzeum
Zamkowe w Pszczynie, Poland

SHELAGH

EIGHT

THE FIRST CORNWALLIS-WEST

William Cornwallis West was born in 1835 to Theresa and Frederick West and he was to be the first to bear the double name. Faithful to her benefactor, Theresa had ensured that her parents' friend's name was included in the succession.

In her biography of William Cornwallis West *Perfect Darling* Eileen Quelch notes that William did not hyphenate his name until 1886 and only changed the name officially by deed poll in 1895. He would then be fully known as William Cornwallis-West; the double name continued until 1951 when his son George, who was the last in the direct male line died, but there remained various descendants through the female line.

In William we have a story which discloses what seems to have been a change in lifestyle. Up to the death of his father he had led a fairly relaxed life. He had been educated at Eton, trained in law and was called to the Bar but he was also a painter of some talent, which seems to have been a skill inherited from his grandmother, Mrs Whitby and her family. He was also a fine sculptor.

Instead of pursuing a career in law he first chose to live in Florence, where he had been born, and where he stayed for some years, no doubt enjoying the somewhat lush lifestyle of the artistic circle. This was all brought to an abrupt end when his father died and his mother said that he should return to take up his responsibilities in managing the estates as his elder brother had already died. George Ridley, in his book *Bend'Or Duke of Westminster,* notes that on departing from Italy William left behind three illegitimate daughters, but the burden of providing for them remained with him, and subsequently with his estate and heir.

This seemed to be the big turning point in his life; almost from then on he was to be fully engaged in all the activities of a country squire and became a solid supporter of landowners' responsibilities, although he was to retain a lifetime interest in art and continued in the family tradition of painting and sculpting.

'Spy' Cartoon of COL. WILLIAM CORNWALLIS-WEST
Captioned: 'Denbighshire'
Published by VBD, 16 July 1892, signed: 'SPY' BR.

Having returned home, William settled at the hereditary seat of his part of the West family at Ruthin Castle in Wales. In due course, he would take on the various positions of Lord Lieutenant of Denbighshire, also becoming a Member of Parliament and Colonel of the local Royal Regiment of Fusiliers. It is somewhat unkindly remarked by Ridley in his biography of the Duke that this last position was of the 'Kentucky' variety, as William had never served in the army, and it merely came with the local titles of office. That may be so, but it did not detract from the dedicated way he subsequently carried out his duties.

William maintained a house in Eaton Place in London, but he was not married. It would not do for someone in his position to remain single. With his well-trained eye for the ladies, shown during his years in Florence, he had no trouble in making up his mind. However, his choice of wife was to be significant and was one with which his mother, Theresa, could not come to terms.

Mary was the daughter of Frederick Fitzpatrick, an Irish vicar with country and county tastes. Mary's mother Olivia, whose father had held office as Lord Chamberlain to the Queen, was from a noted family living near to Dublin. Olivia had a reputation which had led to her being banished from the Court in London to Ireland where she met and married a vicar. They had four children, one of whom was Mary. Born in 1855, Mary was to be known for her entire life as Patsy.

In the 1860s her parents then returned to live in England at Warren Hall in Cheshire. One of Mary's sisters and her daughter Ena feature in this story in later years.

Olivia quickly moved back into the circles from which she had been banished. Although Queen Victoria had become a recluse after the death of her husband Prince Albert, the same gloomy state had not enveloped her son Edward, Prince of Wales. He continued to enjoy an outgoing lifestyle; the gaiety and exuberance of Edward and his circle of friends were by-words of the day.

It was into this world that Olivia and Patsy were to be pitched, and they both enjoyed it immensely. Both mother and daughter were renowned for their great beauty and charming personalities. Aged only sixteen, it was not long before Patsy's youthful prettiness had won over the married Prince of Wales and she in turn fell in love with him. The affair which they started culminated in a life-long relationship and friendship.

To facilitate the affair away from the bright lights of London Patsy needed to marry, so between the Prince and Patsy a husband was sought. Into the scene sailed William Cornwallis-West who was then just taking his place in important society circles, living at Ruthin Castle in Wales, not too far from Cheshire, and looking for a wife. William was captivated by Patsy, he fell for her, irrespective of the manipulative hand of the Prince, and the die was cast which led to their marriage in October 1872.

Throughout his life William showed Patsy a devotion which remained until he died in 1917, despite the well-known love of his wife for the Prince of Wales and other 'interesting' aspects of her behaviour generally. (The Prince of Wales was a not infrequent visitor at Ruthin when William was away on his duties and later the house at Newlands provided another opportunity for Patsy and Edward to meet. Rumours regarding paternity arose at the time of Patsy's various confinements, especially with the birth of George.) In fact, so far as he was able, William strongly defended Patsy from malicious gossip. In 1879, when Patsy and her friend Lillie Langtry were libelled in a London society magazine he took their case to court; the editor was found guilty and sent to prison.

William undertook his local duties very seriously, although these were personally fulfilling, they were also a drain on the family resources at a time when the family landholdings were collapsing in value and rents from any tenancies declining. William had a kindly nature and so it is likely that he did not put tenants under pressure to pay what they could not afford. Instead he looked to develop the land his father and mother had acquired down at Milford in Hampshire.

At Milford, stylish villas were to be built in order to bring the town up to date with a fashionable seafront to rival other smart resorts along the southern coast of England. It seems to have been about then that the place became known as Milford-on-Sea, no doubt to attract the type of people for whom the development was intended. However, progress on the development was not swift and despite the best efforts of a land agent, expenditure exceeded income. It is said that Dick Birch, the Agent from Ruthin in Wales during William and Patsy's time, spent much of his time at Newlands trying to make the development at Milford a success.

The family fortunes continued to decline and were not helped at all by William's son George, now in the army, whose ability to spend money freely was well exercised. This, in due course, was to presage the loss of the family estates.

William's tendency to be rather lax in money matters did not come from his mother's side; there had been no indication of such fiscal slackness there. His mother Theresa, as well as his grandmother Mrs Whitby, had both shown excellent business abilities and their mentor, the old Admiral, had not been one to splash his money around. However, his own father, Frederick, had been labelled as an adventurer, so perhaps that was the inherent streak.

His early years spent living in Florence, visits there with his parents later and his style of living amongst the artistic set in his own postgraduate youth may not have assisted young William's attention to financial matters. It was plainly his kindly nature and generosity which in the following years endeared him to his family, and for which he was remembered by people on his estates and in the county.

The financial pressure on the estate was relieved somewhat when his two daughters Daisy and Shelagh were married off to husbands of substance, although William continued to have the costly burden of his society-loving wife, Patsy, and son George; their lives will be described in the later chapters of this story.

William was not shy of making a few applications for financial assistance from his son-in-law, the 2nd Duke of Westminster, as times became hard, but more will be said of this in the later chapter on his daughter, Shelagh.

William's dutiful life was not a colourful one; the excitement was provided by his wife to whom we shall turn shortly; her chapter relates the twists and turns of her political manipulations which were to get her involved amongst the highest in the land.

The last years of William's life were not to be very happy, as a number of unfortunate events combined to give him a great deal of trouble and concern. These were made even more difficult for him by Patsy as she became mired in serious trouble of her own making. He came to her defence but it was not to avail her greatly.

By the beginning of the First World War in 1914, the financial pressures on the estate were considerable. Developments at Milford had not provided any great improvement and this poor state of affairs continued. The London house could be let, but the not infrequent use of it by the ladies of the family did not make that easy.

George, the spendthrift, continued to be a drain on the family, even being bailed out by his brother-in-law the Duke of Westminster.

The final indignity was the case made against his wife Patsy, when she was in all but actual terms put on trial where her reputation was at stake, and in essence she lost.

William, who was by then not at all well and was spending much of his time painting (art had been amongst the first loves of his life), wrote strongly in her defence in defiance of the many lurid stories in the press but without success.

When William died in July 1917, Patsy was too ill to attend his funeral. This illness had been brought on by the stress of the situation arising from her indiscretions compounded with other ailments from which she suffered.

Efforts had been made to pass control of the properties, Newlands Manor and Ruthin Castle, into the care of the Pless family of William's daughter Daisy. However, that was not to be. Although the papers had been prepared, they were not considered to be valid as George, the heir, had neither consented to the arrangement nor signed the documents. Thus, when William died, all the houses were either sold to pay off George's debts or were seized by bailiffs for the same purpose. Ruthin was sold and at first became a hospital and then in later years made into a hotel; Newlands Manor was stripped of its artistic refinements, which had been added by Patsy, and these were put into auction by the bailiffs along with the house.

William was mourned not just by his family, but by the staff and people residing around Ruthin and at Newlands who remembered him as a kindly and generous man and his life was noted as being one of service; characteristics which are fine when extolled in the time of the bereavement, but which do not live long in the history books. The famous Shakespearian phrase 'the good is oft interred with their bones' in this case is most apropos, although there is no evidence of any evil living after him.

Although William was only an adopted heir to the Admiral, William Cornwallis, it seems he may have acquired some of his more considerate traits through his mother who, as a young child at Newlands, would have experienced the kindness of the old Admiral. William's grandson, Hansel Pless, had a very similar thoughtful and courtly demeanour, as testified by his second wife Lady Ashtown formerly Mary Minchin, when the author had a short conversation with her in 2008.

NINE

THE DAUGHTER IN LAW

Patsy Cornwallis-West was the one on whom most of the family relied for their development, especially socially. Born in 1855 she was baptised with the names Mary Adelaide Virginia Thomasina Eupatoria, so her familiar name of Patsy must have been a relief to many.

Her family background arose from a marriage between Olivia Taylour, who was a daughter of the Lord Chamberlain, and an Irish clergyman, Frederick Fitzpatrick, who was the Rector at Cloone in County Leitrim. Prior to the marriage Olivia had been at Court but had been banished by Queen Victoria for an alleged dalliance with Prince Albert. In later years, after the death of the Prince, the Fitzpatricks returned to England and Olivia slotted back into the social whirl of former times.

At the young age of sixteen Patsy had followed on from her mother, Olivia, in royal family circles and had become a favourite of Edward the Prince of Wales, indeed one of his lovers, as is asserted by Tim Coates in his biography, *Patsy, the story of Mary Cornwallis-West,* something she shared with her close friend of later years, Lillie Langtry.

So close was Patsy's relationship with the Prince that when her son George was born, it was the Prince's solicitor George Lewis who made all the arrangements. Thus the speculation about parentage at the time may not have been without some foundation.

The proximity of Ruthin in Wales to the Grosvenor estates, the family seat of the Duke of Westminster at Eaton Hall near Chester, enabled all of her children to enjoy a close relationship with that noted family, one which was to lead to the marriage of her daughter Shelagh to the 2nd Duke, known as Bend'Or.

However, Patsy, her husband William and their family spent much of their time in London, especially when the children were young for a spell of some five years, partly because of renting out Ruthin for economic reasons, and partly for the social lifestyle; quite apart from which William's mother, Theresa, would not have Patsy to live at, or even visit Newlands, her estate in Hampshire.

The Roman Gardens at Newlands Manor

Later, when William's mother died, Patsy took Newlands to her heart, not solely in the house which she lightened and very much brightened, but in the gardens as well which she developed in a delightful and creative fashion. Patsy's work on the gardens was extensive and the Roman Gardens, are typical of her achievements. Sadly the statues disappeared when the house and grounds were sold off to meet family debts and the problems of George's bankruptcy and they may well be adorning some other garden elsewhere in the country.

The house became the centre of the social circle in Hampshire, the Prince of Wales and his friends being regular guests. This gave the Prince two bolt holes away from prying eyes, one at Newlands in addition to the other at Ruthin Castle.

At Ruthin, Patsy was known in the neighbourhood for her great kindness and consideration towards the local people, who in later life when scandal struck her, stood by her. Years after her death visitors to the area would hear people speaking most kindly of both Patsy and her husband. This must have been a trait which they passed on to their elder daughter, Daisy, as she was to achieve, after her marriage to Hans Prince of Pless, a similar high regard amongst the staff on the estates in Silesia and amongst the workers in this German district for her care and consideration.

In London, the Cornwallis-West family house in Eaton Place was close to that of the Langtrys and the two wives greatly enjoyed the social lives customary in those carefree late Victorian times when the Prince of Wales was still free from the burden of the Crown. However, the death of Victoria was almost a signal for life to change in various ways; the former Prince, now King Edward VII, was no longer so free to enjoy himself as he had done for so many years. The relationship with his nephew, the Kaiser, deteriorated and Edward's health was suffering from the generous indulgences of his earlier years.

All of this was to have an effect, not just on Patsy but on her son and daughters, one of whom, Daisy, was later to be torn between loyalty to her native land and her marriage into one of the principal families in the land with which Britain went to war. To Patsy other problems arose much nearer to home, and which were ultimately to be her undoing.

In his book about Patsy, Tim Coates has provided a full description of the events which were to bring senior members of the armed forces and government into public notice, and readers with further interest would be well advised to read that fascinating and detailed account. For the purposes of this story, a synopsis shows the way in which Patsy eventually lost the hold which she had on events for so much of her life.

If one compares the perception of these circumstances taken by Eileen Quelch, George Cornwallis-West's good friend and biographer in 1972, to that of Tim Coates in 2003 who, in those later years, had the benefit of some documents not previously widely available, the former was inclined to regard Patsy's indiscretions to be of far less consequence, adopting a kindly view of a mature lady who was only trying to assist a young mentally wounded soldier in his recovery. The latter author, in what he describes as 'the true story' of Patsy, relates the events in a more graphic way and the notes which follow are based on that detailed and later interpretation.

Patsy Cornwallis-West's Visiting Card

As might be imagined, it seems to have started with Patsy's fondness for flirtation, in this case not with one of her own social station and maybe that is the reason why it all went wrong.

The sequence of events which then led to Patsy's ultimate downfall started when a young sergeant in her husband's regiment, The Royal Welch Fusiliers, was seriously wounded in battle. Patrick Barrett was one of the very few survivors of the dreadful first Battle of Ypres. Indeed, out of three thousand in that regiment who had started in the war, only eighty now remained and many of those like Barrett were severely wounded and in a terrible state of shock. Shelagh, Patsy's daughter and wife of the Duke of Westminster, had opened a hospital at Le Touquet and it was to here that Barrett arrived after the battle.

He remained there for a while being nursed for his injuries, and some time later, at Christmas 1914, he was sent back home to Wales in order to recuperate in the longer term. He came back to Denbigh and arrived at the home of a Mrs Birch to be cared for, with some other soldiers, before being sent to rejoin the regiment. Mrs Birch was the wife of Richard, the land agent of William Cornwallis-West at Ruthin Castle.

Patrick Barrett was sick, both physically and mentally. He had no zest for life and was well cared for by both Mr and Mrs Birch who had remembered him from his childhood when he was an orphan. He recovered but slowly, and it was whilst he was in this rather indifferent state of health that he met Patsy, the kindly and still very beautiful wife of his Regimental Colonel.

It commenced when Patsy, on a visit to Mrs Birch, met up with the several soldiers housed with her and took them out in her car for a trip into the countryside. Patrick, still very ill mentally remained with Patsy and they talked about his state of health. Afterwards, when Barrett had returned to Mrs Birch's he wrote a note of thanks to Patsy. She replied.

The visits continued and in the various discussions that ensued, it became evident to Patsy that Patrick had hidden within him some greater qualities which merited him being ranked higher than a sergeant. She talked to him about this and persuaded him to apply for a commission, a possibility which would not have existed before the war. She spoke to his colonel to smooth the way for the papers to be made available.

Patrick studied hard at the work which prepared him for the tests he would have to undertake, and in many meetings they had together he received a considerable amount of assistance from Patsy. In addition, his case for promotion was reinforced and supported by Patsy's connections with some senior officers, as well as the Colonel, her husband, putting in a good word for him in the right quarters.

However another relationship developed as in his fragile state of mind Patrick became infatuated with Patsy and she led him on so that, as Tim Coates relates, by the time he achieved his commission they had become lovers. It was from here that things started to go wrong.

On the pretext of being left alone at Ruthin, with most of the male staff being at the war and her husband also away on his public duties, Patsy invited Barrett to visit the castle to undertake some tasks for her and to stay over. The tasks were essentially non-existent and it seemed that they were to serve the passions of Patsy. Patrick became locked into the situation, but his mind was still disturbed and it worried him that he was getting so involved.

It is not evident whether Mrs Birch became suspicious purely out of interest for Patrick's condition, or whether she resented the obvious pull Patsy, her husband's employer, had over this vulnerable young man. After all Mrs Birch, who was younger than Patsy, was a most attractive woman. Furthermore, she had suspicions that her husband was going astray on his several visits to London, which he made ostensibly to look into various affairs of the estates, and that Patsy was conniving in keeping this a secret from her. Anyway, Mrs Birch began to question Patrick and she also raised the question with Patsy as to why she required him to go to the house so many times.

Patsy then became frantic and wrote many notes to Patrick, becoming quite injudicious as some of these were couched in rather intimate terms and sent to Patrick at Mrs Birch's, and even pushed under his door at one time when Patsy was staying at the Birch's.

Patrick was troubled as he juggled between keeping the affair secret and confessing it all to Mrs Birch who continued to question him about the nature of the relationship. Eventually he told her of the true state of affairs. At the same time he wrote a long letter to Patsy which in essence was a plea to put an end to the affair. A second note referred to a suggestion that Patsy had made about the suspected affair between Mr Birch and another woman in London being untrue.

Patsy reacted and took steps to rid herself of the young man who had now responded to being led on by her in a way she could not now bear.

On the pretext that Patrick had taken advantage of her kindness she asked her husband to deal with the matter and as the senior officer of the Command was to visit them they agreed to raise the matter with him. This request was passed on to his Commanding Officer who decided that Barrett should be posted away from the Ruthin area.

However, that officer, on his own initiative, also suggested that Patrick should lose his commission.

As a result of some brusque interviewing by his senior officers at the camp Patrick again became troubled and had another breakdown at the Birch's home where he was still living. By then Patsy had gone even higher in the command structure amongst her social contacts in order to get Patrick removed from the area to another sphere of operations.

The Birches became more involved in the matter, and Mrs Birch especially began to get very angry at what she saw as a great injustice. Mr Birch tried to ameliorate the situation with softening correspondence to Patsy, but this was rather overtaken by his wife's more robust attitude.

Patrick's health broke completely. The recurring effects of shell-shock exacerbated by worry brought him to the state where his transfer to a unit returning to France was prevented by the doctors.

Mrs Birch, becoming angrier, contacted solicitors to take up Patrick's case and for a Court of Enquiry to be held in order to clear his name which she felt had been slurred by Patsy's approaches to senior officers. A letter was duly despatched by them for that specific purpose. Events began to happen in a way which snowballed, reaching the highest in the land, having an effect on the government of the day and the control of the country in the management of the war. Politicians became involved and they used the dissent to their advantage.

A pact was reached between Mrs Birch and her husband over his suspected infidelity on his many visits to London, fuelled by remarks made by Patsy, but which he denied.

Then they set about seeking justice for Patrick. Her husband was the letter writer, but Mrs Birch was the main power and push behind the campaign. Patrick became the tool between the two women as they fought out their respective positions: Patsy defending her reputation and Mrs Birch defending her charge, although there were some innuendos made that her interest was more than one of a nursing carer.

Mrs Birch made visits to see senior officers at the Ministry and as a result of an approach to the local Member of Parliament in Denbigh, who felt that for knowledge of the family reasons he could not take direct action, she was referred to a very respected and diligent MP, Arthur Markham. Markham spoke directly to Lloyd George, the incumbent Minister for War. Lloyd George had political designs against Herbert Asquith, who he regarded as incompetent as Prime Minister and in his leadership of the war.

The case being put forward by Mrs Birch extended beyond the way in which Patrick Bennett had been treated personally to accusations of manipulation of some high ranking officers by Mrs Cornwallis-West, which if taken to any wrong conclusion could be detrimental to state security. It was suggested that communications between a civilian, however noted, and those in command of the forces of the country were inappropriate. A very senior officer, the Quartermaster General Sir John Cowans, was one person named as being directly involved.

Lloyd George could clearly see that taking up the case would support his view that Asquith had poor control, not just over the war but over his ministerial officers and their military functionaries. Markham died quite suddenly of a heart condition, but Lloyd George carried on and pursued the case. This was to the extent of having a question raised in Parliament and the passing of an Act which permitted an enquiry to take place behind closed doors.

The enquiry, in fact there were two connected enquiries, duly took place, but that is the only time that the Act, which permitted civilians to be interviewed and questioned in military matters, has ever been used. One of the enquiries was specifically in the case of Patrick Barrett. It took place in the Guildhall, London.

The verbal exchanges in the tribunal proceedings, with each side seeking to undermine the credibility of the other, on the one hand sought to suggest that Mrs Birch's case for Patrick was really antagonism by that lady, perhaps even jealousy, against Patsy; the contrasting point being made was that Patsy had acted in a bad way towards Patrick, taking advantage of his mental vulnerability due to shell-shock.

For five days the enquiry into the case of 2nd Lieutenant Patrick Barrett continued. His own sworn statement was read to the court as he was too ill to attend. Those questioned in the witness box included Mrs Birch, General Cowans, General Mackinnon, Mrs Cornwallis-West and Lieutenant Colonel Delmé-Radcliffe, the latter as Bennett's commanding officer coming in for particular questioning into his alleged haranguing of Bennett in front of other officers. The tribunal listened to a considerable amount of evidence during the investigation.

At the conclusion of the enquiry, which was preceded and accompanied by a variety of newspaper articles 'second guessing' the various aspects of the case, there was a short interlude prior to the announcement of the decision.

Asquith was put on the spot to answer for his faith in General Cowans, and a report into the failure of the Dardanelles venture was let out at the same time. Political matters came to a head, Asquith resigned and much to the King's distress he had to ask Lloyd George to form a government.

The thought of Lloyd George and Churchill together, both reputed to have welfare reformist and socially inclusive tendencies, was not one which endeared the upper levels of British society to their cause. The war, however had to be won, and the two were to prove to be the team to get the work done, lifting Britain from a dire situation. Undoubtedly the Churchill family's American connections helped to bring that country into the conflict, thus aiding Britain both financially and militarily.

Lloyd George, the arch manipulator, made sure that the report of the enquiry which he had encouraged and put in place continued to act in his best interests, and the releases of the report were made so as to gain maximum benefit for the good of the new government.

Whereas General Cowans was remarked on as being very indiscreet and not behaving in the best of manner, no hard criticism was made of him and he retained his post, one which was vital to the war campaign.

Patrick Barrett was given credit for his qualities as an officer and no blame was laid at his door for what had occurred and it was clearly stated that the censure he had received was entirely unjust. He was personally advised of this finding. After the war he became a teacher, but sadly he was only 40 when he died, no doubt hastened by his war traumas.

Lieutenant Colonel Delmé-Radcliffe was severely criticised for his behaviour to Barrett and his own inappropriate contact with Patsy and was left to face the consequences of his actions.

The Birch family, husband and wife, were considered to have been correct in pursuing the matter on behalf of Patrick Barrett and in bringing it to the attention of the Army Council, although some of their allegations against certain people, notably General Cowans, were felt to be somewhat unjust. Nevertheless their outcome was positive.

But Patsy was firmly and totally discredited, her behaviour throughout being most roundly condemned; it was even being remarked that continuance of her holding any position of importance in the community was a matter of regret. The press had what can only be termed as a 'field day'. The solitary defender of her now sullied reputation was to be her loyal and devoted husband William, who issued a long letter to the press. Her friend Stella also stood by her, although George, Patsy's son, was greatly distressed at her actions and had little contact.

As to Lloyd George, he got credit for seeing that a matter which affected the military had been quite properly and speedily investigated and brought to a fair conclusion.

It could well be argued that the opprobrium heaped upon Patsy at the time was the detritus of the political wrangling between Lloyd George and Asquith. If not wholly so, it is likely that some of the results of those days' manipulations ended up on Patsy's shoulders.

That being the case, the more kindly view of the events taken by Eileen Quelch may not be misplaced, but Patsy's last years of life were not the bright and carefree ones of her youth.

There was no Prince Charming to woo her; her son virtually ignored her and in any event went bankrupt; one daughter, Shelagh, lost her son and heir which contributed to her divorce by the Duke of Westminster. Her other daughter, Daisy, had an unhappy marriage and was isolated from England due to war. William suffered poor health as the result of a car accident and died in 1917.

After the loss of all the houses and estates, due to George's bankruptcy, Patsy went to live with her sister Min, who was married to Guy Wyndham and lived at Clouds in Wiltshire. In October 1919 Min died, and Patsy's two daughters Daisy and Shelagh turned to help her. Daisy, who was in a turmoil of her own with her very strained marriage to a German whose country Britain had so recently been at war, came to her aid. For a while Patsy lived with her in Cannes in a small villa but Patsy had cancer and she returned to England, first to a clinic in Eaton Square for an operation, and then to the home of an old friend living in the New Forest at Arnewood, which had previously been part of the family estate near to Newlands, where she died in July 1920.

Her life had been a colourful pageant ranging from the carefree days of her childhood, through a close relationship with the Heir Apparent to the throne and for many years at the very hub of the high-society of English life. Those days were already beginning disappear by the turn of the 19th century and really started to die with the onset of the First World War, never to return. Patsy's son and daughters and their issue then lived through some of the greatest years of social change into a second great global conflict which finally triggered the end of such times.

By the turn of the next century vast numbers of the great houses had vanished under the demolition hammer. For those which remained it was often only by courtesy of the National Trust, English Heritage and the paying public. Many which had been part of the life of Patsy and her friends would have been subject to that change. Ruthin Castle survives as a hotel, Newlands as apartments.

Detail from the memorial cross in Milford Churchyard to 'Patsy' using her proper name, Mary, with date of death 21st July 1920.

TEN

THE GRANDSON

George Frederick Myddleton Cornwallis-West was born in 1874 on 14th November and duly christened, the son of William and Patsy. There were rumours, however, that William was not the father and that Edward, then the Prince of Wales, might have been be the sower of seed during one of William's absences on duty away from the main family home at Ruthin Castle. The Prince had been an active admirer of Patsy since she was only sixteen and her confinement with George was organised by the Prince's solicitor, as has already been recorded in the chapter about Patsy.

Various writers since have expressed an opinion on the credence of this suggestion of George's paternity one way or another but it has not been substantiated and must therefore remain an item of mere gossip.

The more recent commentators tend to decry the rumours of former days and the truth of the matter is now well buried in time with those who lie with the memories.

As so often happens when parents, especially fathers, are kindly and tolerant, the children grow up with a rather sunny view on life. This was certainly so with George as his own book of social reminiscences *Edwardian Hey-Days,* published in 1929, shows that to be the case. He lived life to the full despite problems with his health until sadly he was afflicted by Parkinson's disease in his later years.

In spite of his happy disposition, George suffered from some indignities and bullying at school which marked his earlier years and these were not helped by the attitude of his mother.

When George went to his first school at Ruthin at least one incident caused his mother to allow the schoolmaster to deliver him a good caning, which he took very badly.

No matter what may be said about Patsy, she probably loved her children. However, that did not really show in her attitude at the time as the task of bringing them up was passed on to the domestic staff, whilst she continued to exercise her love of parties and social visits. What time she did spend with them certainly affected their later relationships in adult life. It seems that hers with George was not good and he felt that neglect deeply. In later years he recalled that for some misdemeanour as a child she had locked him in a dark cupboard under the stairs. In Patsy's later troubles it was to be George who was the most distressed by them and the least forgiving.

During George's early years at Ruthin there would have been a tension between Patsy and her mother-in-law, Theresa, who kept the house at Newlands firmly out of bounds to Patsy. When George was only about two years old, his father had to rent out Ruthin Castle in order to recover some losses as the rents from the Ruthin estate were negligible due to the agricultural depression. They lived in London at Eaton Place and it was to be about five years before they returned to Ruthin.

George described their London family house as being one of unremitting gloom, the inside being lit only by minimal gas lights and the outside much the same with the addition of the almost perpetual smog of those days. The return to the country was a delightful relief from London and the family took full advantage of the life available to them, especially around Ruthin and neighbouring Eaton.

In modern terms, the children might have been considered to

be 'spoilt' because of their background, but the evidence indicates that they were not over indulged.

However, George was to live a very carefree life for many years as he indulged in his almost wastrel-like habits of gambling and then later in speculative business ventures with dubious partners.

George was also an addict of all sporting activity, fishing and shooting being paramount. His secret ambition was to drive a train, and he had the chance, when he was preparing for the army, to help the driver of the local trains in Wales, thus learning a skill which he put to good use in later life when serving in the Boer War, as well as later on when a national train strike affected the railways at home.

For education, George was first sent to Ruthin Grammar School and then via a suitable prep school onwards to Eton College. His university education was at Freiburg in South Germany where, with the original aim of being a diplomat, he went to learn languages. However, that was not to be, as his parents decided that he should join the army and he was appointed to a commission in the 3rd Battalion of the Royal Welch Fusiliers. He was by then too old to enter Sandhurst so he went instead to Camberley Military Academy to learn the skills of military leadership before taking the various examinations and being gazetted into the Scots Guards in 1895.

Life for an officer in those days was not over strenuous so far as military commitments were concerned. In George's own words in *Edwardian Hey-Days*, he records matters around then:

'The life of a young office in the Foot Guards in my time was very pleasant – soldiering was not taken too seriously...'

This enabled him to have an extremely sociable life style, one which undoubtedly led him into and developed the habit of spending money beyond his means.

Several times he was bailed out by his father with money which could be ill afforded, as William too had a somewhat *laissez-faire* approach to financial matters. William was rather kindly to those tenants in difficulties and insufficiently businesslike to those with whom he had dealings in his development at Milford-on-Sea. It may well be a case for 'like father, like son', but the son seemed to take matters to a greater extreme.

It is to George's great credit that in his middle years he wrote the only biography of the man who endowed his own grandmother with his name, wealth and estates, Admiral Sir William Cornwallis. That volume remains as the only definitive history of the life of a very much under-publicised, but distinguished sailor who assisted Nelson in one of this country's greatest hours of need, and who had also served the Crown in the Navy for almost half a century.

Together with a third book written by George on fishing, they form a useful insight into life in Edwardian times amongst the upper social circles.

George's career in the army, after a period of what can only be described as messing around in London enjoying the social scene, took him to Ireland.

By his own admission, the life of a commissioned officer in that country was one of total enjoyment of the various social and sporting activities and that any military activity beyond basic parades and some simple manoeuvres were the least of the officers' worries. In *Edwardian Hey-Days* he describes these pleasant diversions and quite happily records how young officers would depart from military affairs for a day's sport, leaving the sergeant majors in charge.

He later served in South Africa in the Boer War where he became better acquainted with Winston Churchill. This connection was further strengthened in 1900 when George married Winston's mother, Jennie, the widow of Lord Randolph Churchill who was the younger son of the Duke of Marlborough. However, there has been more than a little suggestion that George's departure for that field of conflict might have had more to do with the events leading up to that marriage than would have otherwise been the case.

These events were to try the determination of George and Jennie, as in neither case were the respective families keen on their forthcoming marriage, indeed the Cornwallis-Wests were far from happy and neither was Edward, the Prince of Wales.

It seems to be fairly well accepted that both Patsy and Jennie had been lovers of the Prince. There was also a twenty year age gap between George and Jennie. Jennie already had two sons, Winston and Jack. One rumour of the time was that Jack was the result of her union with the Prince, although other possibilities for paternity amongst her closer male friends were mentioned, as for a period she was isolated from Lord Randolph who lived more often away than at home. Again, there does not appear to be any proof for the speculation but one is left wondering why more was not done at the time to scotch such rumours. The failure to do so undoubtedly set suspicious minds wondering.

At one point, both Lord Randolph and Jennie had been estranged from the Prince as Randolph had offended him. This resulted in Randolph being despatched to Ireland in 1877, to act as an unpaid secretary to the Viceroy, his father the Duke of Marlborough. It was not until 1880 that Jennie and her husband were able to return to England and six years later that the Churchills and the Prince were reconciled. Although Jennie and the Prince resumed their friendship, Randolph was not always part of the social scene.

The relationship between Jennie and George arose from a meeting at Warwick Castle in 1898 when both were guests of Countess Daisy of Warwick, reportedly another lover of the Prince, who was also present. George was then only twenty four. It has been further suggested that his presence might have been as a result of Jennie noticing him at a previous event and her hostess obliging by inviting George.

The two struck up an immediate friendship. From George's point of view the daughter of an indulgent and rich American father may have been an attraction, and for Jennie the prospect of inheriting by marriage a home in a stately castle in the heart of the British countryside might have been interesting, but it seems that they must have had a deeper affection for each other at the time. However, it has been suggested that Jennie was inclined to chase after any virile young man, and certainly George fitted into that category well.

Their courting was not to be comfortable. Although Jennie was attracted to the young man, it was he who led the chase, writing a great number of passionate letters. Jennie seemed to be satisfied with the physical side of the relationship as lovers, and did tell George that there would be no marriage, but that did not deter the young man. George continued to bombard her with letters of love and passion.

Although his father pointed out that the relationship was quite inappropriate and his mother totally disapproved, George remained in his world of love, even making himself ill with his passion. The Prince told Jennie firmly that he did not approve of the relationship but it continued in a way which, even in those rather care-free days, was something of a shock to the rest of their social circle.

After a year Jennie's strong will to avoid marriage was weakened and the couple talked about an engagement. This really set everyone against them. George was lectured by the Prince, who could see that Jennie consumed by passion for George would not otherwise be readily available to him, that a marriage to someone so much older than George would not be satisfactory.

Jennie was considered by friends and others in the royal circle to be very foolish to consider a permanent union with a young man known to be so loose in his financial habits, especially in view of the very considerable age gap. Winston himself, although not being in favour of the marriage, showed an early sign of his diplomacy by refusing to be drawn into the family row.

So the South African war intervened and by a combination of efforts from Patsy, Jennie, George's commanding officer and the Prince of Wales, George was given a posting to the war zone as ADC to Lord Methuen who was to command the 1st Division. At this time Jennie herself had some qualms about committing to a long term relationship with her lover, therefore she was not averse to him being sent away to test the bond. At the same time she put pressure on her contacts to arrange for her son Winston to be accredited as a War Correspondent, and he also sailed for the Cape.

However, Jennie did not stay at home in England; she obtained a ship to be used as a hospital and took herself off to the war. In this project she was aided by her family and her sisters who helped to raise the money necessary to fund the hospital ship. The project was finally secured by the gift of a suitable ship by an American who defied the general trans-Atlantic opinion which tended to support the Dutch settlers against the might of the British Empire. Jennie thus got her way and it was not long before she was anchored at Cape Town.

The adventurous family group would have been complete when Winston's younger brother Jack also decided he would head for the same conflict, a matter of great concern to Jennie, but that was not to be. Before Jenny set sail, George, after a few adventures of his own, was to be invalided home with what could today be described as post-traumatic stress and consequential illness following a severe bout of sunstroke. Despite frantic cables home for her to wait for him, Jennie had already left with her mercy mission when George sailed for England. It was at this time, too, that Winston was captured but later made his well-publicised escape.

On his return home George was admonished by his father for continuing with such a foolish notion, threatening a break with his family if he carried on with his proposal of marriage to Jennie. George continued to maintain that it was marriage he wanted, even though his commanding officer told him that he would have to resign his commission. Although George challenged this particular demand, after consultation with other senior officers, he decided to go on 'half pay' and thus on to the reserve list from which he was not to return to active service until 1914.

After six months of separation, Jennie returned from South Africa still very passionate about George, although not firmly decided on marriage. However, with her two sons looking as though they were to be married and the prospect of a solitary home, Jennie let her heart rule her head and the engagement to marry was announced.

The wedding took place in Knightsbridge on 28th July 1900 and, despite the great misgivings of so many of their society friends, the church was host to a goodly crowd of the aristocracy. The bride was given away by her late husband's father. The Cornwallis-Wests did not attend, a matter which gave George much sadness. There were twenty years difference between wife and husband, he being twenty six and she forty six.

No children came from the marriage which endured until 1912 when they separated, finally divorcing in April 1914, when George re-married.

George's life with Jennie would be coloured by the fact that she also had a penchant for spending money. Her upbringing as one of the five spoilt daughters of a wealthy American family had been her foundation in this habit. During her earlier marriage to Lord Randolph and while with other lovers she had managed to keep herself in comfort financially. Although it is not knowingly recorded, George's inability to provide unlimited funds may not have greatly assisted the smooth process of their marriage in the very extravagant years of the Edwardian era. In addition, Jennie's way of becoming involved in productions and charity functions which could be spectacularly successful, even if costs exceeded expectations, was not one which assisted his financial state.

Through Jennie's contacts George was introduced to the life of commerce. Eileen Quelch, in her biography of George entitled *Perfect Darling*, describes how Sir Edward Cassel got him placed with the British Thomson Houston Company where he received training before being appointed as its chairman and of other associated companies based in Glasgow.

However, Charles Higham in his biography of Jennie, *Dark Lady*, deals with the matter far less kindly by describing George's position as being one of a 'semi-glorified clerk', comparing that unfavourably with the position Cassel put in the way of Jack Churchill in the City of London. Be that as it may, the fact is that George had a job to go to for this period. The way in which this was viewed according to the perception of writers is not to be debated here.

Their permanent home became Salisbury Hall near St Albans where Jennie arranged social events which George attended with her on his visits from his work, mainly at the weekends. They thus lived semi-separate lives. This suited Jennie as she continued to show a very keen interest in Winston's career which she tried to assist either by direct campaigning or pulling various strings amongst her many contacts.

Still a relatively young man, George could not really settle down to serious business as his heart lay in the sporting world. To be fair to him, however, according to Eileen Quelch he did make a reasonable fist of his tasks in Scotland and was quite kindly regarded by his colleague directors and those employees with whom he came in contact. However, his latent desires for the finer things in life and not too much responsibility remained, of that there is no dispute.

Everything from the fine old traditions of country pursuits to horse racing and then sports cars interested him. At this age, he still had an eye for the pretty girls and they for him. Insofar as Jennie was concerned, although they still had a passion for each other, she was beginning to show her age, not so much to those of her own generation, but to a younger man with his best years before him, the difference was plain.

Within a few years some cracks began to appear in their relationship and five years later there were very definite strains. It became obvious that Jennie could not hold George's attention from the younger ladies. After year or two George decided that the safe formality of the business boardroom was not exciting enough and left the position which had been engineered for him by Cassel.

He entered into partnership with another, a Mr Wheatear, their joint purpose being to promote investment in new businesses. The first year was relatively successful, but thereafter it was not to be plain sailing and affairs took an unfortunate turn.

This failure in business was to haunt George, as in 1907, with the run on banks in America, his own enterprises suffered very badly and his health took a downward trend. The family baled him out, but significantly it ended up by George and Jennie giving up their home at St Albans and moving to London.

A later entry into a business deal with a crooked lawyer who used the money, which had been provided to pay off debts, for his own purposes and which then left George with even greater problems caused his health to break down completely but it seemed that Jennie still showed great concern for him.

However, it was one of his wife's enterprises which lead to the final break in this marriage. Jennie had promoted a play *Borrowed Plumes* in which the leading lady was Beatrice Patrick Campbell, the noted actress whose husband had been killed on active service. Before the play opened in 1909, George and Beatrice had fallen for each other and it was soon very evident that was the priority for George. He spent less time with his wife and more with Beatrice, who was more widely known as Stella. Charles Higham in *Dark Lady* comments that Jennie engineered the work George had to do with Beatrice, thus throwing them together, as she had reached the limit of her patience with him.

In 1909 George moved away to a house at Cavendish Square in London and it is evident that he spent time with Stella. *'I met many interesting people at Stella's charming little house in Kensington Square'* are words from *Edwardian Hey-Days*. In this he also refers to meeting George Bernard Shaw and J M Barrie. With the former he was to form and continue a friendship which lasted many years.

Earlier, Jennie had turned to her sons for advice and comfort and she also wrote to Patsy about her deteriorating relations with George. A letter from Winston to George starkly set out the options and procedures for any formal disentanglement of their financial affairs. Winston also wrote to his mother encouraging her to proceed with the appropriate steps to separate their lives.

Jennie set herself the formidable task of staging shows, one of which at Earls Court had led to her being considered as an impresario of some note at the time. Artistically it should have been a great success but the activities, which included acts of jousting, did not always go as envisaged. The show ended up far from being successful. Most significantly it did nothing for her finances as it lost money.

George criticised her for her flamboyance and inability to make any money out of these hugely notable and what should have been successful ventures. This must surely have been an example of 'the pot calling the kettle black' as George had shown little ability to get his own financial house into any form of good order. He singularly failed in showing financial responsibility by developing a propensity for gambling, whilst his wife scaled these grandiose schemes the costs of which usually outstripped the income.

Many years later, in one of his ventures into literature, it is suggested that he rather poorly disguised one of his characters in the work; his model for his text seemingly based on his former wife Jennie, being treated in a disparaging way.

George's marriage continued to deteriorate, the two drifting further apart and inevitably they decided that separation would be the only option. Jennie was typically generous in the spirit of the way she dealt with the matter, according to Eileen Quelch, and offered George her best of good wishes for his future once the proceedings for divorce were on their way.

The decree absolute came through, after the tortuous passage over two years, and Jennie was equally generous in spirit in her final letter to her former husband, making it plain that if he ever felt a need to call on her for moral comfort he would not be turned away. Plainly she still held a great deal of affection for him.

The day after the divorce became absolute George married Stella Patrick-Campbell.

Jennie was to marry again in 1918 to Montague Porch, a man twenty three years younger than herself.

After suffering from a fall, the wound went gangrenous and this necessitated the amputation of Jennie's leg; as a result of a sudden haemorrhage, Jennie died on the 21st June 1921, aged only sixty seven. George mourned her loss and said he had made the 'greatest mistake in his life' by parting from her.

It was only two years after his marriage to Stella in 1912 that the First World War turned the life of nations upside down, never to be quite the same again. A whole way of life changed, and the social revolution which had been simmering for years across Europe finally boiled over.

In the few weeks before the war broke out George had made his own preparations by purchasing a new uniform and when the day came he joined his unit then assembling in Kensington as a reservist. He remained a lieutenant, as he had been when leaving active service in 1901. However, George was not to remain in that rank for long.

Churchill, as First Lord of the Admiralty, had decided to strengthen the army by use of the surplus Royal Navy's reservists in the formation of a Naval Division. This was made up of two naval volunteer reserve brigades and one of the Royal Marine reserves. He was short of officers with military discipline and experience and looked for transfers from other units. As a Guards reservist who had seen active service, albeit not for many years, George saw an opportunity and he volunteered. He was accepted and was put in command of the Anson Battalion, named after the Admiral of that name, and stationed at Dover.

His task was to train the reservist sailors into soldiers, rank and file and officers as well, which was a task to tax the abilities of the teachers and pupils alike. In those days there was no demand for any training to be done by reserve officers, so by the time the war started, George's own military ability had not really advanced from what it was in 1901.

There must have been more than a few like him but, whatever may be said about their state of training, no-one could doubt the bravery of the young officers who led the troops in that war. It is just sad that so many lives were lost at all levels by the lack of skills and modernisation.

Nevertheless, some sort of order was achieved and by October 1914 the units embarked for Antwerp to take part in the fighting. On arrival they were put to defending the city by digging in at the suburb of Vieux Dieux. The chance of firing their weapons had been minimal prior to departure and the units were not well provided for in equipment, so they were not best equipped for their task. It was not to be long before the enemy was bombarding them in their inadequate entrenchments.

The Belgian troops around the area had equally inadequate artillery to respond. Their communications were poor and at one time according to George they succeeded in shelling their own positions. The German forces continued to advance and it was not long before the British had to retreat in order to extricate themselves. By forced marches and some assistance from buses most of two brigades managed to make the coast and be shipped back to England, but one brigade was cut off and captured and spent the rest of the war in captivity.

George was in one of the brigades which made it back home but it is remarked in Randolph Churchill's biography of his father, Winston, that George had berated the demoralised troops during the retreat. It is also noted in the same volume that in correspondence Asquith had been rather less than complimentary about George's capabilities, although as this could be due to the total lack of training undertaken by reserve officers, it could have been somewhat unfair to single him out for specific criticism.

The units may have been pitched into a task for which they were unsuited, but the tactical ploy of trying to hold on to Antwerp had been successful. The holding of the German forces to the task of gaining the city had won the British valuable time elsewhere, and Sir John French had managed to move his forces to Flanders, which later stayed the advance by the enemy upon the Channel ports. That area was then to be the centre of major operations during the future years of protracted trench warfare.

Back in England, it was not long before George was working at the reorganisation and training of his unit at Blandford, in Dorset, where new recruits were being enlisted to replace those lost or injured or otherwise being re-drafted back to naval duties.

It was then that the tolerance which was part of his nature came to be tested by imputations that he was a spy or at least in sympathy with the enemy. His family's known German connections (sister Daisy was then married to the Prince of Pless) fuelled the wildest of rumours which even began to be printed in newspapers in America where his wife Stella was appearing in a play. One report actually gave an account of him being shot as a spy.

George's health was never too robust. The winter between 1914 and 1915 was very severe and he was laid low with bronchial problems, exacerbated by worry. As a result of a medical board he was granted six months leave. George spoke to some of his senior officers who agreed that it would be good for him to go to America to refute these stories, at the same time suggesting that he could act as a listener to gather up any information as to how the Americans were reacting to the war. Some of the reports coming to England indicated that public opinion was not all necessarily supporting the British case. There was considerable sympathy being shown for the Dutch Boer colonists.

On arrival in the United States he was soon meeting people, especially in clubs of a sociable nature and some incidents gave him the opportunity to discredit the view that Britain was the 'bad guy' in the conflict. In addition he gave several interviews to journalists in order to put over the Allied cause and case. His progress was assisted by the popularity of his wife Stella and he was able to capitalise on her social connections and made good use of them in his task, a combination of British propaganda and fact finding.

George travelled widely in America, including having a break for a fishing trip to recover from yet another bout of illness. In due course he returned to England where he reported back on his various findings, including a discussion which he had with the ex-president, Roosevelt. He then returned to his reserve battalion for military duty, making a request to go to the front and he was posted accordingly. However, his health was still in very poor order and he was classed as being unfit for active service and so was appointed as Assistant Provost Marshall based at Hounslow near London.

George spent two and a half years in that post which had the curious outcome of allowing him to continue with a fairly sociable lifestyle as one of his major tasks was to root out any idle officers who were dodging their military obligations. His duties also included the responsibility of ensuring that officers in the district were of good behaviour and dressed in the proper way. Inevitably this meant that his social connections were well extended during this period. That is not to suggest that he did not undertake his task in a proper manner, just that he was well placed to do so and, at the same time, being able to enjoy the privileges of the finer points in life to which he was accustomed.

At his own request at the end of the war, instead of being immediately demobilised, he was at first heavily engaged in ensuring that tendencies to mutiny by soldiers who had not been demobilised were repressed. He was then sent on the same duties in southern Ireland. He was discharged later in the year retaining, as was the custom in those days, his rank of Major by which he continued to be known in the latter years of his life.

His business interests had by then collapsed, partly because a dishonest banker had lost him some £8,000, and he did not have the money to support an extravagant lifestyle. His first efforts at writing had not helped his financial situation at all. The circumstances at Ruthin, with staff mainly at the war and rental income minimal, did not allow his father to bail him out. In fact, although George and his brother in law Bend'Or Westminster were estranged at the time, it was the latter who aided him with a loan secretly made through Winston Churchill. This gesture was one which did eventually bring about reconciliation between George and Bend'Or.

As a result of this poor state of affairs, some cracks began to show in his marriage to Stella and even during 1916 Stella had some discussions with his mother, Patsy, as she was very concerned that any actions against George could affect her own position. If George's finances were so bad as to render him bankrupt she did not wish her own assets to be seized and the idea of divorce had to be considered. It was then that Patsy disclosed to her friend that, as a result of George's improvidence and in order to safeguard the family properties, the two premises of Ruthin Castle and Newlands Manor had been secretly put into a trust in the care of her daughter Daisy and her husband the Prince of Pless.

Within a very short time, actually during that year, George was indeed made bankrupt. The record showed that he put down his own extravagant lifestyle as well as that of his first wife, Jennie, as being part of the problem. The rest was down to the failure of his business efforts, too many of which were speculative and that he had been failed by a dishonest solicitor.

The view of the official receiver was that he had lived beyond his means, had been very rash in his speculation, and that such extravagance had inevitably led to the final bankruptcy, stated at £170,000, a considerable sum in those days.

His father William died in 1917, before the war was over, and the estates became George's responsibility. He was not to enjoy them at all as the validity of the trust set up was questioned and overturned and the bailiffs moved in to collect their dues against the debts racked up by him. In any event, the family estates were not in the best of financial health due to the very poor state of the economy which had prevailed for some years.

Ruthin was sold and the money used to alleviate part of the debt in bankruptcy. Newlands was seized and everything there was sold to pay off more creditors.

In the years after being demobilised, George had a difficult time. His income was negligible and although still married, he was in effect without a wife as he and Stella lived apart. For a while he made himself useful in the task of looking after a child of a friend in the country who had died, but his main base was only to be a room at the Guards Club.

Although the marriage had broken up, he and Stella did not divorce as she would not agree to release him from all the debts he owed her. In the intervening years before she died in 1940, Stella made sure that he paid back all he had borrowed. Stella remained a friend of Patsy until her death in July 1920.

George never forgave his mother for the shame he felt she had brought on the family by her behaviour in later life on top of the rather hard and unfair way he felt she had treated him during his childhood.

By 1920 there was nothing left of the family's estates, but George had cleared sufficient of his debts by then to be discharged from the bankruptcy.

George was now able to acquire a house in Sterling Street, London, near to Montpelier Square. This house really became a living museum of his records of his family and he was served by a couple as manservant and cook/housekeeper. Having thus settled himself with a base George commenced to use his talent as a writer. He had inherited from some ancestor, possibly his grandmother Theresa, or her mother Mrs Whitby, a talent for writing. He first tried plays, but with little success. His books were more successful as his style was easy and readable and they included two volumes dealing with some aspects of his life and associated matters.

His *Edwardian Hey-days* is an absolutely delightful insight into the way of life during those years, from his birth in 1874 up to the First World War and shortly afterwards. It is not an autobiography in the full sense as it is not a continuous narrative. It does not detail any matters relating to his marriages and divorce, although it presents some aspects of their associates and lifestyle. It certainly emphasises the gentrified existence he continued to pursue despite his very poor financial state.

His most notable achievement in writing was *The Life and Letters of Admiral Cornwallis,* his biography of his 'ancestor', the man who, in a way, originated the Cornwallis-West name. The book was published in 1927 but unfortunately for George he was not to gather much benefit from it as the publisher failed almost immediately after the book was printed.

George was aided in his literary efforts by his acquaintance with George Bernard Shaw, almost as part of a triumvirate with Stella who was greatly admired by Shaw as well, although between the three of them there was a tense relationship. Their correspondence was considerable, albeit with some long gaps in between, especially by Stella. There is no relevance here to refer to the relationship between Stella and Shaw; that is a story which can be taken up by reading any publications of the actual letters and related commentaries.

It is claimed that Shaw even rewrote some parts of plays which George originally penned. Certainly there were many letters, some of considerable length, giving advice on the style and length of the pieces which George had written. Extracts from some of Shaw's letters are included in Eileen Quelch's biography of George. Despite this assistance, George's plays were not very successful, although some kindly observations were made by some of his correspondents.

The years rolled on through the 1920s and into the 1930s with George producing his books and plays. The income derived from them was never large but he seemed to live in modest comfort, keeping up with friendships and managing to continue with his outdoor sports and a fair deal of social activity with his established titled friends. As with Shaw, he had no illusions as to the outcome of the rise of Fascism in the 1930s and the outbreak of the Second World War would come as no surprise.

When Stella died George remarried; his bride was Georgette Hirsch, the widow of a South African gentleman. They were married on the same day that the memorial service was being held for Stella, almost replicating the pattern of his divorce from Jennie and his marriage to Stella earlier. The newlyweds did not live in great style, their circumstances were indeed modest and George's indifferent health continued to be a burden. However, by undertaking some public duties in lecturing to units of the Home Guard, he managed to get a small fuel allowance which helped him to remain mobile.

The heavy air bombardment forced George and his new wife out of London, and they sought a quieter life, ending up in a hotel near Bournemouth at Branksome. There he managed to undertake duties to assist in the war effort, and at the same time he was reasonably placed to try his hand at a bit of fishing in the nearby rivers. It was not until the war had ended that the couple returned to London, not to his house, but to rooms which they rented.

It is to his great credit that during the Second World War years, despite his being handicapped by a lack of wealth, health and mobility, George became very active in promoting the case of his nephew Hansel Pless who lived in England and who, ostensibly for the security of the nation under Regulation 18b of the Defence (General) Regulations 1939, was taken into custody as an enemy national. Hansel was released after three years of imprisonment, with an apology that this had been a mistake and the order was revoked, but he bore no grudge against his adopted country and the home of his mother.

George otherwise, in these latter years after the war, lived an uneventful life and this was made miserable by ill-health and the onset of the progressive Parkinson's disease. This he endured until 1951 when he rose from his sick-bed, took a pistol from his desk drawer, and ended his own life.

To be fair to him, although one might criticise much of George's lifestyle as being empty and wasteful in comparison with current ways, it was no more so than for so many other young men of the period. The last few years of the Victorian era at the height of British colonial power were extravagant ones for the upper classes, and the waywardness of the Prince of Wales and his lush lifestyle exemplified this. In those same years the social upheavals amongst what would then be considered to be the lower orders became more aggressive and by the First World War that structure of society as it had been ordered for many generations, was well on its way to collapse. Aggressive socialism and communism took over.

Militarily, despite the setback of the two Boer Wars, British power remained supreme until the outbreak of the First World War in 1914. It then became apparent that our armed forces, at least on land, were not at all well trained to cope with modern tactics. The officers were very brave as they led 'over the top', as were the soldiers who followed them, but the many years of failure to move from the gentlemanly habits of the former era were insufficient to hold the day against a much better trained force. It took the input of the new military power in America to sustain Britain in those times.

By his visit to that country George did make some contribution in bringing the Americans together with the old country in their war against the territorial aggressors.

George Cornwallis-West was a product of those years, and some older members living in the early twenty-first century will recall from childhood seeing quite a lot of elderly and moustached military gentlemen who lived in modest circumstances. Frequently they would be known as 'Captain this', or 'Major so and so', and a fair number lived in small seaside hotels where their subsistence was partially covered by some sort of service they provided acting as hosts for the other paying guests.

George Cornwallis-West was not one of these, but his final years must have indeed been considerably more modest than the relatively care-free years of his childhood and of his youth when he mixed with the highest in the land. He was very much a man of his time in those early years, but by the outbreak of the Second World

War and the aftermath when the social orders he had known finally broke down, he was a man out of his time, and he knew that.

It is perhaps not difficult to see just why, after so many years of social jollifications amongst the rich and famous, and much freedom of sporting activity, that he would particularly feel the restrictions brought on by his illness and the future would look black indeed. The taking of his own life must have been a desperate act, borne out by the hopeless position in which he found himself, with an ever reducing ability to enjoy himself in any way, as had been his custom for so many years.

In her biography of George Cornwallis-West, his friend Eileen Quelch has dealt sympathetically with her subject, the rather bare bones of whose life are given in this shorter synopsis. Those who seek to read more would do well to seek out a copy of *Perfect Darling*.

The Times summed up his life in the obituary published on 3rd April 1951:

'Moving as he did in the very centre of Edwardian society (his father was a great grandson of the second Earl De La Warre and two of his sisters became respectively Princess Henry of Pless and Duchess of Westminster), he was led into an extravagance he could ill afford. An attempt to retrieve his fortunes in business proved unsuccessful… It is, however, by his deftly crafted books of reminiscences of the society he knew so well that he will be best remembered.'

Perhaps that is as fine a memorial one could expect, for a man who enjoyed life, loved the ladies, and served his country, albeit that his senses of financial responsibility were less marked.

So with that thought in mind it is time to move on to other members of the family, which was known to Edward, Prince of Wales as 'The Wild West Show'.

ELEVEN
PRINCESS DAISY

Born on 28th June in 1873, and baptised as Mary Theresa Olivia Cornwallis-West, but popularly known in the family and thereafter as Daisy, she was the elder of the two daughters of Patsy and William. The other daughter, Constance, better known as Shelagh, was the third child of the family, George being born between them.

Daisy was widely renowned for her childish prettiness which translated into teenage beauty that survived for many years as she matured into adulthood. Unhappily, the torments within her life and increasing infirmity meant that her latter years were to be very disturbed and by the time of her death she had been reduced to being a reclusive patient cared for by a devoted helper and friend.

An incredibly full story of her life has been compiled by W. John Koch in his book *Daisy – Princess of Pless, A Discovery*. That, together with George Cornwallis-West's book *Edwardian Hey-Days*, has been helpful in trying to compile this shorter study of her eventful life.

Daisy herself wrote copiously, and her diaries together with other commentary amounting to four volumes issued between 1894 and 1936, with an edited version in 1950, provide a considerable close insight into her life and times. Koch's book was also inspired by experiences from his life as a child in Silesia, Germany, in the early 1930s when some of the older residents had memories of Princess Daisy and her charitable work amongst them. As a detailed account of her life it would be hard to find a better work which commends itself to anyone whose appetite may be whetted by the following pages.

The purpose of this chapter is not simply intended to relate Princess Daisy's experiences, but to try to link her life with the rest of her family who remained in England at least so far as domestic living was concerned, albeit that they visited her in Germany during her marriage to the Prince of Pless.

Daisy had three sons by the Prince, and their lives were to be torn apart by the two World Wars, and their somewhat unhappy tales are related in the later chapters of this book.

George Cornwallis-West plainly looked up to his elder sister for moral help in his childhood when he was at the receiving end of what he considered to be very unfair treatment at home or at his preparatory school. The responsibility she showed was to continue throughout her life when she did so much, against all the odds, to help reduce poverty in her husband's homeland of Silesia.

Edward the then Prince of Wales, who was closely associated with their mother Patsy and therefore met the youngsters many times at Ruthin and Newlands, nicknamed them 'The Wild West Show'. It was not just an interpretation of their childish or teenage behaviour, as it remained their *soubriquet* for many years after that.

However, in 1891 Daisy broke away from the relative comfort of that childhood and at the age of 18 she married an incredibly wealthy heir to one of the oldest and major titles in Silesia, the land which bordered Germany and Poland, where the territorial challenges by both of those countries kept it in a constant turmoil of nationalistic and political fervour.

Although born at Ruthin, within a short time the children were decamped to London with their parents, for serious economic reasons, where for five years they lived the routine life of typical metropolitan family, being taken to the parks for outings by nannies, or shown off to important visitors at the house, or kept out of the way of their glamorous mother and compliant father. George remarks on the gloom of that existence, not just in physical terms of dingy lighting and dark streets, but in the rather colourless traditions of those entrapped in London for more than just the 'season'.

Daisy Corwallis-West
From a painting by Reginald Arthur
Courtesy of The Milford-on-Sea Historical Record Society

The return to Ruthin was a release from that life and it gave them all an opportunity to indulge in the open air activities of the countryside which they all enjoyed. Later, on the death of their grandmother, Theresa West, they had the benefit of Newlands in Hampshire which had been bequeathed by Admiral William Cornwallis to their family. It is related that Daisy as well as her brother and sister had considerable pleasure in exploring the charm of the gardens which their mother set about embellishing, and in the additional facilities provided by the area and the land owned by the family up to the coast at Milford.

These were the happiest of years for Daisy but it was not very long before the rather more formal atmosphere of a very aristocratic German life took over.

Patsy was determined that her daughters would marry well and in this she certainly succeeded. She could not, however, predict how those marriages would develop. Was Daisy's a forced marriage? Well, perhaps not so in the way such marriages are arranged within certain customs, but in a less forceful way it appears to have been so.

In the first place Patsy had made sure that any teenage admirers of Daisy had not been encouraged so that when it became her turn to 'come out' in London, she was a new star in the firmament of young ladies to be admired.

In that respect she was a show stealer, as not only was she a very beautiful woman but also one endowed with a charming yet impish personality. In addition she had developed a maturity in ways and conversation which was not an attribute in all the debutantes. The latter may well have been due to the way she and her siblings had largely been left to be brought up by staff at their homes, although that was not unusual amongst those in the landed classes. At any rate she was popular and well sought after.

That was not enough for Patsy as she sought out the very best for her daughter. There may have been some selfish interest in her desires as well as for her daughter, as a marriage into a family with wealth would be of advantage. The Cornwallis-Wests were less well provided for than they had been when the Admiral endowed them, as

Patsy had not been backward in spending, and the old Ruthin family estates were not the best providers of income due to the depressed state of agriculture. Additionally, the development at Milford-on-Sea was proving to be more of a serious drain on the family coffers, instead of providing some useful income.

It was not long before the right person came into Patsy's sights: a thirty year old German noble coming from a good family with a seriously important title and who benefited from a substantial income from mining and industry. He was Hans Heinrich, heir to the Prince of Pless who was reputedly the wealthiest person in Germany.

Patsy set herself out to gain this remarkable prize for her daughter. She succeeded, and it was not long before the fathers of the two families met together to agree the match and make the financial and nuptial arrangements.

Rather unkindly the Prince of Pless called for sight of several generations of the English bride's family tree to be produced, but this was to be no problem as the Wests could trace their ancestry through the De La Warr line back to the Black Prince in the 14th century.

Much more importantly was to be Daisy's relationship with her new husband. She had not shared her mother's enthusiasm for the match. She had voiced some opposition to the arrangement as she was certainly not head-over-heels in love with this rather severe person who was more than a decade older than her, and she had said as much when he proposed to her. Indeed she had her eye on a young man from another peerage.

To Hans Heinrich, who it was reputed had been sent to London to match with Princess May but lost her to the future George V; this match with Daisy was a second choice. None of these matters augured very well for the future, but Patsy prevailed and the marriage went ahead.

Daisy would be one of so many young ladies who, in those times, bowed to the wishes of parents and reaped what they had sown. In many cases the marriages were extremely happy, in others quite the opposite. In Daisy's case it became a sort of halfway house where neither love nor animosity succeeded. Certainly as she went through the wedding ceremony at St Margaret's, Westminster, on December 8th 1891, and at the lavish reception afterwards, Daisy's mind was not filled with the love of the moment, but more in hope that, as her husband had suggested, some would develop as life proceeded.

Hans Heinrich XV
Courtesy of Muzeum Zamkowe w Pszczynie, Poland

That life was not to be aided by the situation which arose as a result of the two nations' relationships breaking down and ending up in a destructive war. She was to survive that but the marriage would not do so.

John Koch, who in his book about Daisy quotes from her diaries, illustrates her feeling at the time of the marriage, and her first months of her new life. Her first experiences in Paris, where they stayed after the wedding, were very mixed. On the one hand the attitude of German men was much coarser than she had been accustomed to amongst her English friends; on the other hand she enjoyed being the centre of attention at the German Embassy where her husband and she were shown some deference. On balance, by the time the honeymoon in Paris came to an end Daisy was in a better frame of mind and looked more positively towards her future life at Pless. She had even decided on an English nickname for her husband, Tommy, which he agreed to allow her to use.

However, it is appropriate comment that Daisy never really got to understand the rigid formality of the German ways, and that her life was to be a constant battle between that and the far more relaxed ways of the English aristocracy. Her sparkling personality was not quelled although it was not always accepted by her new relations and their associates. One major exception was to be her father-in-law '*Vater*' with whom she developed a great relationship and later another was Kaiser Wilhelm who became her protector against any animosities espoused by the State, especially when the world war aroused such unpleasant feelings.

After her marriage, Daisy's life can be broken up into three sections: from the marriage to the outbreak of the First World War, the wartime period and afterwards up to her divorce and then the years thereafter. It is useful to consider each of these periods separately.

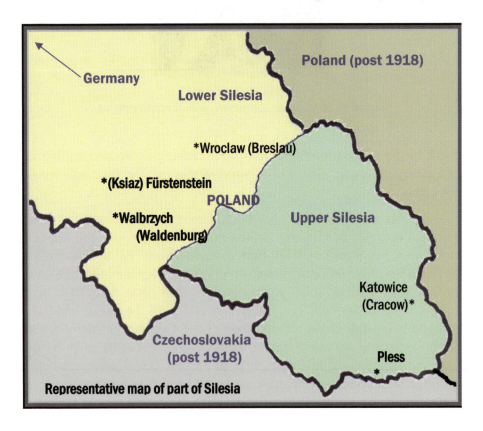

Representative map of part of Silesia

There were three main castle residences within the Pless estates: Pless, Fürstenstein and Waldenburg. Hans Heinrich XI, Count of Hochberg and Duke of Pless, the Fürst and leader of the family at the time of their marriage, lived at Castle Pless and it was to there that Daisy and her husband, Hans, travelled after their honeymoon.

The map illustrates the geography of that part of Europe, Silesia. It should be noted that parts now known as Poland were in Russia pre 1918 and Czechoslovakia was part of the Austro-Hungarian Empire before 1918. Silesia was argued over by Russia, Germany and Poland.

It is interesting, however, to note the amount of travelling undertaken by members of her family over the years, not only in Germany but to England as well. The time taken in journeys and the distances did not make them any less likely to visit their friends and relations, although the length of stays in any one place may have been longer than would now be the custom.

Daisy's attitude had become more positive and she now looked forward to meeting her new relations. In this she was to be very disappointed as they tended to talk amongst themselves, with the exception of her father-in-law, and Daisy with her little knowledge of German often felt excluded. The stiff formality of German upper-class living she found stifling and the omnipresence of staff flunkeys was overpowering. It was difficult for her to do anything for herself as uniformed door openers and closers stood in every room. In England it had been the custom for staff to be sent for as and when required. In her new home they remained an adornment all the time.

However, Daisy and Hans did not continue living at Pless but moved into the rather brighter castle at Fürstenstein which had been renovated as it had not been lived in by the family in any major way for some years. It was here that Daisy set about the task of settling into her marriage and trying to make the best of her life in a strange country.

In the first place, the newly married couple received a very warm welcome from the local people who wanted to see the castle livened up by family living once again. In this they were not to be disappointed as Daisy made it her habit to visit the town and move amongst them, and in due course with her care for their conditions, she became a firm favourite amongst the staff and townsfolk.

Daisy had been the liveliest of the Cornwallis-West children and it was not in her make-up to be serious and gloomy. Her spirit could easily have been quelled by her new life but she fought against this in a variety of ways. One of these was to try to engage the staff in normal conversation, such as she might have done in England, although this was strictly against the 'house rules' which had been laid down by her husband.

In other ways she allowed her sometime quirky sense of mischief to dictate her actions, and John Koch records the occasions when even her tolerant father-in-law was inclined to advise her as to the wisdom of some of her actions. She had certainly caused him some concern as she rebelled against some of the traditional ways of dress, as she did not care for many of the drab 'uniforms' which the ladies were required to wear on certain occasions.

Her husband was indeed very fond of her, but the formality of the ways in which he had been brought up and educated made it very difficult for him to show his inner feelings and Daisy felt this very keenly.

Daisy was not alone in suffering from the different customs and ways of life between the two countries. Much earlier on, in 1858, one of Queen Victoria's daughters, also Victoria, had married Frederick who was later to be Emperor of Prussia, and they did have a happy personal marriage but then she was widowed and lived alone other than for her house staff and any guests. That part of her life was not so happy and she felt alienated from the very people amongst whom she lived and especially had problems with the Chancellor, Bismarck.

It happened that the Prince of Wales had foreseen the problem which would affect Daisy and he asked Victoria the Dowager Empress of Prussia, his sister, to look out for her. An invitation duly arrived for Hans and Daisy to visit her. It is difficult to see who benefited the most from the visit, Daisy or the Empress, as they equally poured out their troubles on to each other's shoulders.

It was a visit which had a mixed effect on Daisy, as she also had to take the burden of the various cares of the former Empress. Nevertheless, it probably helped her in a way by realising that her own problems were not unique amongst those who married between the different cultures in Europe. By the end of the visit she may have been weary of her hostess's problems, but she was better equipped to manage her own.

However, much as a result of this visit as of any other factors, Daisy was to benefit in a wider way by the friendship which then developed between the Kaiser and herself. This was partly due to the Dowager Empress's influence and also because of her own personality when she later met him on a visit to Berlin. Although the Kaiser was later to be at war with Britain, Daisy's home country, his attitude to her throughout the friendship was always one of utmost respect for her.

Daisy's visit to the court at Berlin with her husband in the very early years of their marriage was to project her into a circle of friendships and contacts which later she used, almost ruthlessly, to help her in the social work she took up to benefit the poor and needy.

It was to be three years after her marriage before Daisy next visited England, in 1894, and that was to be the start of a year of travels and visits which covered most of the ruling houses of Britain and Germany, as well as those of the lesser aristocrats who mixed in the same circles. It was during this series of visits that Shelagh, Daisy's younger sister, took to accompanying her. Shelagh was then her constant companion for several years until she too got married. Her husband was the 2nd Duke of Westminster.

During these travels and visits, the Prince of Wales had met Daisy on several occasions. He was a man with a perceptive mind and it had soon become obvious that Daisy was not very happy in her marriage. It was then that he offered that she and Hans accompany him on his forthcoming trip to India. Quite apart from the adventure of such a journey, this particular part of Daisy's life was to provide her with the mature self-confidence which superseded the rather girlish responses to the pressures on her shown previously.

After Daisy experienced a miscarriage, she sailed for India with Hans; she had still not acquired an understanding of her husband and his family so she was feeling very 'down' in health and spirit. The journey and visit were to change her whole attitude and bring to her an inner strength which then stayed with her for the rest of her life, helping her through her marriage and in her later social work, in politics when she tried extremely hard to keep the peace between the two rulers of England and Germany and in business ventures as well.

The visit to India was not without interest in its own right, but first she had to get there and she proved to be a rather poor sailor in the hotter climates, so she had to go into hospital when they arrived in Colombo. That delayed their tour until January 1896 when they set sail for Madras. Their onward trips with the Prince were then to take them overland, first to Calcutta, across country to Bombay and then on to Hyderabad.

In her diaries of the time Daisy recorded disappointment at the very limited amount of time she had to see the real India, as their Royal host was more inclined to mark his tour by visits to places of entertainment, such as the various horse race tracks and the houses of the various important people who had the expensive task of providing for him and his entourage.

Socially, Daisy had to take care of herself for quite a long period, especially when her husband went off on a tiger shoot during their stay in Calcutta. This brought her close to the Maharaja of Cooch Behar who many years before when visiting Newlands had fallen for her, then a gorgeous fourteen-year-old and blossoming into a young lady. During a visit to his palace he made it quite plain that he still had strong feelings for Daisy but she managed to show that, although she admired him, her life was with her husband. However it did not escape the eye of the Maharanee that her husband was infatuated with Daisy, and their marriage, which had been under some strain for some time, broke up with much acrimony.

Daisy had to travel by train across country to Bombay to meet up with the Prince and Hans and during this time she confided her deepest thoughts regarding her life to her diary. She even composed some poetry of a romantic nature. It seems that this long period on her own must have given her time to settle her mind as to her future.

The paradox of her relationship with her husband, who on the one hand expressed his devotion to her, but on the other then left her for many weeks in this strange country whilst he went off on men's enjoyment, must have given her food for deep thought. She must have realised that their whole ethos of life was basically different in so many ways and that this would be a problem for their future years together.

It certainly seems that on this visit, when she had time alone, Daisy came to some form of peace within herself and an acceptance that the life which she was to lead with her husband would be one of tolerance of each other's ways, and that visual expressions of love were not part of the character bestowed in Hans. This was to be the mainstay of their relationship for the next few years of their life together, and certainly until the outbreak of the First World War.

Unlike Daisy, who had been brought up in a world of interest, be it art or the country life, Hans had little interest in such matters, even his aptitude for what might be termed political work in his country was quite low. Indeed he had not been called upon to exercise any talent in that direction and later in life Daisy had to push amongst her contacts to get him noticed and appointed to some office.

However, one matter which did set him afire was the plan he had to develop their home, Castle Fürstenstein, in a very grand way. In this Daisy was to support him, not necessarily for the building, but later in the way she would be the hostess.

These, apart from her childhood times at Newlands, were to be the 'golden years' of Daisy's life, relatively speaking, and in which she was to blossom into an elegant and exciting hostess. This was then followed by a period in which she showed a serious interest in social welfare and, later on, considerable political activity in trying to reduce tensions between Britain and Germany in the final years leading up to the Great War.

Hans's plans for the development at Fürstenstein were grand to say the least. The construction works were so extensive, that in order to accommodate the guests who they invited there, a luxury hotel was built nearby and Daisy exercised her considerable talents in decorating it to very high standards.

In this art she had no doubt been trained by her mother, Patsy, who had spent so much of her time, talent and her husband's money on Newlands Manor but the financial constraints on Patsy were not a worry for Daisy as her husband's family resources at that time were almost unfathomable and were available for the development work. At least they were within the bounds set by Hans's father who was less carried away with the plans than was his son, but after '*Vater's*' death funds were directed in vast quantities to the project.

Daisy set about politicising herself, at least to the extent of trying to get her husband a public appointment to fill in his time when he was not otherwise engaged with his building works. These efforts were not limited to contacting the senior people in the local nobility who still led the administration, as she made appeals to Emperor Wilhelm, the Kaiser, with whom she had developed a very close relationship.

In her efforts, she was partly rewarded when the Kaiser sent Hans as a special envoy to the United States to open the German Trade Fair in New York, and he did well at this; the press remarked how well he and President Roosevelt had got on socially but her further ambitions for him to be appointed to the embassy there or later as the First Secretary in Paris were not fruitful. As a friend pointed out to her, Hans did not have the training nor natural talent to hold such an office, and she had to agree that his character did not lend itself to such political and administrative work. Even locally, her efforts to get him placed in office as President of Silesia were not to succeed.

During this period of their lives both Daisy and Hans travelled extensively both on the Continent and to Britain. Many members of Daisy's family and those into which her brother and sister had married were to become regular visitors to Fürstenstein: Shelagh and the Westminsters and Jenny Churchill, now married to brother George, enjoyed the hospitality and the lifestyle. George, in particular, fell for the outdoor gaming pursuits and relates details of some adventures in his memoir, *Edwardian Hey-Days.*

Successful socialising with the German aristocracy was not to be so readily achieved due to their cultural differences and antipathy prevailed. In fact there was even outright hostility to Daisy with her enthusiastic socialising ways, which caused her some distress.

Perhaps one of the main objections that the local German aristocracy had was that Daisy and Hans introduced into their home and entertained visitors from so many other countries, not just Britain but from Austria, Hungary and Romania. In addition there were the leading people from the multitude of princely states which had been subjugated to the new German nation on its formation in 1871. Even though the individual territories may have been reduced into pieces of a larger jigsaw, the titles still remained in a meaningful way, and the holders still had significant social status. This remained the case until the German revolution in 1918 when they lost out to the State and thus became titles with little or no power.

Over time the opposition was broken down and eventually some of their aristocratic neighbours in Silesia relaxed sufficiently to enjoy themselves. As a relief from those strains, some visits into neighbouring Bohemia provided a change as the air of formality was left behind.

Certainly, Fürstenstein was at the hub of a very extravagant social life at a time when the first stirrings of serious social unrest were showing themselves across Europe. It was to be the background of those uprisings which later was to bring Daisy into one of the most fruitful parts of her life, as she saw at first hand how badly so many people were treated as a result of exploitation.

For the moment, however, the emphasis was to be enjoyment of life, and two of her sons were born, Hans (Hansel) in 1900, then Alexander (Lexel) in 1905. The later birth of Bolko in 1910 was to be a great medical trauma for Daisy, inflaming a circulatory problem which was to stay with her for the rest of her life, putting her into a wheelchair in her final years. That son, Bolko, was always a sickly child, became no stronger in his adulthood and he died, still only a young man in 1936.

In the period from the turn of the 20th century to the political unrest, which preceded the outbreak of war, a dozen or so years later Hans and Daisy became probably the most noted of the many hosts amongst the circle of titled people and other aristocrats who spent their time visiting throughout Europe. Castle Fürstenstein became the paramount social entertainment venue with balls, receptions, and garden parties being almost continuous when the two hosts were in residence.

Daisy also widened the scope for entertaining the workers in the family businesses far more than had previously been the custom. For Daisy it was not sufficient just to have presents for them handed out at the local municipal offices; she instituted a procedure whereby they were invited to come to Fürstenstein to a suitable reception or party where they would receive their gifts.

SOCIAL WORKER DAISY

The first two decades of the 20th century was also the time when Princess Daisy launched in to her social work. This brought a great deal of criticism from the other aristocratic families in Germany as she extended her work and operated beyond the hitherto recognised limits of staff and workers connected to the family. Her inspiration may well have been her mother, Patsy, whose concern for the staff at Ruthin in Wales was well known. Indeed, despite her other problems, Patsy was highly regarded by the ordinary country folk of the district, her compassion for them being legendary and remembered long after her passing.

The Pless family, through the head of the family, '*Vater*', had been so very much to the fore in looking after their workers with favourable living conditions, a special shop (akin to a modern day supermarket) and many other benefits which kept them happy. It is interesting that despite the colossal expenditure on pomp in the several households the workers did accept that, taking almost a pride in the affluence of their patrons.

Hans Heinrich XI, 'Vater'
Courtesy of Muzeum Zamkowe w Pszczynie, Poland

Daisy, however, had made it her business to visit other parts of the area, especially the town of Waldenburg, and saw at first hand the deplorable conditions in which so many ordinary people lived. Quite apart from the poor, indeed slum, housing there was inadequate sanitation with the local river being an open sewer. Disease was rife, and early deaths from typhoid illnesses were commonplace. Such was the state that the stench which arose from the river affected the castle itself and the family at times moved away until it diminished. It was said that Daisy did not just rely on others to seek out the problems, but that she took herself off to find out what was wrong.

She then set about harassing officials to do something about the problem, constantly putting pressure on them by contacting the leading politicians in the regional offices of government. Daisy did not restrict her activities to the local notables, she went to the top and in 1903 at the Kiel Regatta she tackled the Kaiser and Chancellor von Bülow. As a result of this direct approach things started to happen but even then it was not until five years later that the project was started at Waldenburg. It took another five years to complete.

The very full social life at Fürstenstein did not prevent Daisy taking more interest in the people of her adopted country; indeed it seems that Daisy may well have utilised some of the contacts she made in the social round to help her in her charitable work. Certainly she was not shy of trying to prise out support from amongst the rich and famous of her time, and perhaps some might have been taken by surprise to be used for such purpose, but on the whole Daisy got what she wanted in the end. The river drainage project was one example.

Another aspect of her care related to the children of the working families, where she found a high level of physical handicap. Additionally she found that only a very small number of children had any education after fourteen. They went into the mines or to other labouring jobs, with no opportunity for betterment.

Assisted by one of the directors of her father-in-law's mining companies in Pless, Daisy set about the founding of a school to deal with the cripple children which also included their onward care well into their future lives. She and her co-founder Herr Schulte visited the factories in the district in order to set up places for the children to learn real skills when they left the school and not just to be sucked into an under-class of labouring for a lifetime at meaningless tasks. John Koch records that the school opened in 1907 and for many years Daisy kept raising funds for its continuance.

Daisy also looked to alleviate the problems of mothers trying to make ends meet and who were stuck in a cycle of birth, childcare and work. Before long she had persuaded the churches to get involved in improving the lot of mothers and children. Mother and baby clinics were started and milk clinics were another product of her prodigious energies. Thanks to the churches and Daisy's efforts, a new attitude towards the lives of working class mothers and their children was developed.

In her work Daisy was mainly supported by her father-in-law and at times by Hans, but in 1907 '*Vater*' died and Hans entered into a period when his personal extravagance brought great differences in attitudes between him and Daisy. Although their lives had been quite strained at many times since their marriage, the death of his father released Hans from any inhibitions he may have had, and he set about achieving a dream.

He now had the flow of money from the mining companies in his hands and this enabled him to pour resources into developing Fürstenstein in very elaborate ways. No money was then available for Daisy's charity work so whatever she had inveigled from Hans in the past, as well as from his father, came to an abrupt end. However, Daisy continued with her work.

It was during this period of the castle reconstruction that Daisy became involved in some of the internal work at the hotel which Hans had built in the nearby town to house all those guests who would otherwise have stayed at the castle. This extravagance by Hans rather changed the attitude of the workers who had so loyally respected his father, a man who in the ways of the times had shown them care and consideration and lived in a modest fashion. Although Hans survived the revolution in 1918 it was not due to any credit achieved by his philanthropy. Daisy was, however, remembered with devotion by the people right up to her death.

During the re-building of the castle, renovation was not the right word to describe the extensive works, Daisy set out on a business venture which was to change the working lives of many women, and bring back to life a craft which had almost died.

Mechanisation of weaving and like processes had virtually killed off the handiwork of the Silesian lace makers in an area of the country outside Fürstenstein. The factories had attracted the women to work at the new looms, dropping their hand skills, but an economic crisis in the earlier part of the 19th century had closed down many mills, throwing the women out of work. Efforts by the rulers of the day failed to attract the right kind of investors to revive the lace making, only those who sought gross personal profits. The industry was in a dire state as any goods produced were bought by handlers who took the profits, leaving almost nothing for the women.

Daisy, who had long admired what little lace was available, took up the baton of helping them after a visit to the area where she met a lace maker who worked from home. Together with two other ladies who had started to improve the situation with a new lace school in 1906, she set out to develop her own outlets. She opened one lace school after another, until by 1912 she had fourteen of them, including ones which she bought from the other two ladies involved with her.

She was achieving her aim of changing the operation of what had remained of the industry from a basic capitalistic system where the workers had been exploited by the 'middle men' to one of co-operation. The profits were turned back to those whose fine skills brought the demand, either by pay or re-investment to improve processes and working conditions.

Daisy opened shops in many of the fashionable towns and cities throughout Germany and she attracted the support of the Empress. It was an achievement which expanded Daisy's work as a reformer of the lives of women into areas beyond the locality around Pless, Waldenburg, and Fürstenstein. As the businesses developed and wages were paid to the workers from the profits, this brought forward more women into this craft work and the skill which had been lost over generations revived. It was an achievement made entirely by her singular approach and her determination to do right for the people of her adopted homeland.

DIPLOMATIC DAISY

The death of King Edward VII was a considerable loss to Daisy. He had been her friend and indeed her close *confidante* and safeguard for so long in her life. John Koch relates circumstances just before the time of the King's death when he visited Daisy's elderly grandmother, Olivia, and had asked her about her relationship with Albert, Queen Victoria's husband, quite openly. Such was rumoured at the time when Olivia was sent away from the Court circle. The Royal rascal obviously derived much pleasure from his enquiries which he probably felt reflected in his own lifestyle.

To Daisy, she had not only lost a dear friend, but a line of contact which had helped her in her attempts to conciliate between the rulers of the two kingdoms, Britain and Germany. Almost from the time when she first went to Pless with Hans after her marriage, Daisy would be involved, sometimes only in minor ways, to bring better relationships between the two related, but separate Royal Houses.

King Edward had constantly been irritated and frustrated by the attitude of his nephew Wilhelm but Daisy had done her best to reconcile the two adversaries and keep lines of communication open between them. When Edward had visited Germany, Daisy was part of the supporting entourage, together with her husband, and this must have assisted to promote some harmony between the two monarchs.

After Edward's death, Daisy had some contact with George V, his successor, but there was no warmth in the relationship as there had been with Edward and her political communications were to be with the notable or senior nobility with influence in government.

First, it must be recalled that in January 1871 Germany was a new country which under Bismarck had thrown off the over-pressing hands of the Austria-Hungarian and the Second Napoleonic empires. Bismarck was now its Chancellor and Frederick, the Crown Prince of Prussia, was created the First Emperor. Frederick was the husband of Victoria, the daughter of Queen Victoria of Britain and their son and heir was Wilhelm.

Frederick was a progressive monarch and it is probable that had he not died when he did, the ensuing years of the century and beyond might have been quite different. As it was, however, on his death Wilhelm succeeded to both the Prussian and German Crown as the Second Emperor. It was not long before he dismissed Bismarck from office and there is a notable picture of that event showing the sacked Chancellor 'leaving the ship'. In the period after his accession Wilhelm showed a rather aggressive tendency, possibly brought on by an inferiority complex. This strained the old established relationships with Britain.

However, he also had the task of maintaining unity within the new Germany and presenting it as a strong country with a position in the world, especially in Europe. Although the diplomats could see that he was not averse to peace, his pronouncements to strengthen his people and to promote the new country carried certain tones of sabre-rattling which created unease.

The bruising defeat of German colonial ambition in North Africa when the European nations formed up against Germany for her intrusion into Morocco, hitherto recognised as a sphere of French influence, was a first break in the harmony which had prevailed for many years between Britain and Germany. Although there were some calming voices in the Reichstag, the fact remained that a rebuff had been made which offended the people, and the more right wing media capitalised on the situation to stir up unease between the two countries.

Daisy, in the first years of her marriage, had had to accustom herself to the differences between the two cultures, now she had the problem of trying to maintain a form of peace between her royal sponsor, Edward, and her new found protector in Germany, Wilhelm. The latter had come about from the warm relationship which had arisen between Daisy and Victoria, the Kaiser's mother, and despite the ensuing war was to remain so right up to the time when Wilhelm went into exile in 1918.

Edward VII had shown little patience with Wilhelm, regarding him as a pompous upstart who was always trying to push himself forward as the leader. He did not like his nephew and it showed, not just between them personally, but in an attitude from Edward to the Germans in general, so that serious tensions arose far beyond the Royal houses. Aspirations of the people of the new nation to have a greater influence in affairs of Europe and the world started to become more obvious.

Daisy decided that she must do something to try to alleviate the growing hostility and so she set about her work using the unique position she had as a prominent link between the two countries. In major manoeuvres and other less military events such as hunting parties and balls she made it her task to bring together the political leaders of the two countries. Winston Churchill was one of those she introduced to Wilhelm, and in London she befriended the German Ambassador, Metternich.

The Embassy had become a base for Hans and Daisy when they visited England and, as the Ambassador had no partner, Daisy became the hostess at the German Embassy in London and in that position she organised a lot of events to bring together influencers of political opinion in the two countries. Sadly Count Metternich did not take up all the opportunities which came his way from Daisy's efforts, and it seems that he failed to report on these to his superiors in Berlin.

If all this political activity seems to be rather curious, it has to be recalled that the House of Pless was one of the foremost families in Germany, in regular direct contact with the Kaiser and the other leading people of the day. By that alone it was not unusual for Hans and Daisy to be a part of so many events, social or otherwise, and Daisy was not slow to make the most of the opportunities so offered, even without Hans who for much of the time was taken up with his development at Fürstenstein.

This also came at a time when Daisy was still struggling with the cultural difference between herself and her husband, which she saw as a reflection of the wider differences between the two nations; so she found it almost a mission to try to bridge that gap. In both her marriage and in her many political efforts the results were not to be successful, but it can scarcely be said that she was to blame for the ultimate break in both instances.

One of the problems which continued to raise difficulties was the almost continual 'bear-baiting' between the people of the two nations. The media did not help, as it was quite commonplace for cartoons which made some mockery of the King to appear in the German press, and the English papers were not slow to caricature the Kaiser. It was in this framework of constant niggling criticism that Daisy continued to try to ameliorate between the two monarchs. John Koch quotes from a long letter sent by Daisy to Wilhelm in which she almost pleads with him to send some softer message to Edward VII. In that letter she points out the faults in the characters of the people of the two nations but says that they should still be able to maintain peace between the two countries.

In a no less robust way she also wrote to the King, but by then he was declining in health and had developed an almost fatalistic view about the state of tension between the two countries. It was not long before he died and Daisy lost contact with the one person she felt could help her in her efforts to maintain peace.

In Germany, although the Kaiser acknowledged the passing of the King with a period of court mourning, the press corps was less helpful in their remarks, and they did nothing to calm, even slightly, the rising state of tension between the nations.

The period after Edward's death was depressing for Daisy as not only was the tension between the two countries rising, but her marriage was deteriorating. Her sinecure at the German embassy in London was finished as Metternich was dismissed by the power players in Berlin, and replaced by an arch exponent of German prestige seeking, Baron von Bieberstein. He did not last long in post as he became ill and died within a few months of his appointment. Prince Lichnowsky succeeded him and as a personal friend, Daisy was to find him most helpful in trying to head off the growing tensions between London and Berlin.

Daisy's next involvement was with the diplomats, including Lord Haldane, Baron von Stumm, Lord Rosebury and Sir Edward Grey. It was the latter whom she tried to prod into action to accept an invitation from the Kaiser to visit Germany, but which approach he claimed not to have received.

Until the actual outbreak of war, Daisy took up the case of ameliorating between the two nations at every conceivable opportunity, be it at social or formal gatherings. Her contact with the Kaiser was continual, often bordering on the tactless as she tried to be robust in her comments. The Kaiser's obsession with building a navy was mentioned in one instance as that activity was only serving to encourage the British to expand in a like fashion.

Towards the end of this long and drawn out pre-war diplomatic period Daisy almost switched her entire tactics from the basic pleading for toleration to a new front which put forward the idea that the real cause of the situation was social unrest. In this she may not have been wide of the mark. She had prepared documentation together with Sir Arthur Crosfield which proposed disarmament by the nations with the dividend of a peace bonus being put to social and welfare reform. Without doubt, the proposal was to avoid war by another route; that all the aggression was caused by the desire of the nations to improve the lot for their people and could be reduced by settling the social unrest which was causing the misplaced ambition.

It is interesting that this early document, which was frustrated by the assassin's shot in Sarajevo that finally set the war in action, could be seen as an early attempt at developing a wider European community concept. It took two large-scale wars and huge destruction on all sides before the same idea emerged much later in the 20th century.

In the document, Daisy and Sir Arthur recognised the danger of Russia and its instability, again an advance picture of future events. John Koch remarks too on the link between the proposals made by the two authors and events which have been taking place almost half a century later in his book on Daisy.

Although Daisy was in Britain just before war was declared, by the time war broke out, she was back in Berlin. The day before the declaration of hostilities she telegraphed twice to King George V, requesting him to intervene to prevent a final breakdown between the two countries and stop any declaration of war by Britain. It was all too late, pride had taken the place of reason and the war which brought about the greatest change in social conditions broke out on August 4th 1914.

It is suggested that Hans was surprised that Daisy had made her way back to Germany in the days before the declaration and that he might have been better pleased had she decided not to do so and to stay in England. Certainly it was not to be easy for him in the years which followed, as others in the German High Command were not happy about his English wife, and made that obvious.

The years of the war were to provide Daisy with many new challenges set against the background of changes in Germany which were to bring about the downfall of the Kaiser and the collapse of the autocratic rule of the old families, to be replaced by the ambitious politicians and militarists.

During the war she was to spend long periods away from the family homes, separated from Hans who had a great fear that her presence as an Englishwoman would aggravate the tense situation at Pless, which had been turned into the main Imperial Headquarters, and create problems.

Later in 1914, Daisy, living in a hotel, worked at a hospital in the Tempelhof area of Berlin. Hans had asked her repeatedly to go to Fürstenstein but Daisy felt that working for the Red Cross would keep her much better occupied but she was constantly criticised by many of the military leaders and the press had a field day in printing stories about her, that she was a spy for Britain.

Foolishness on her part in visiting a prisoner of war camp with her brother-in-law unfortunately provoked a huge outburst against her which brought about orders for her to be sacked from the hospital in Berlin. It took a long time for that matter to be smoothed over having been suggested that Daisy had breached the goodwill of her Red Cross position to be a spy and in the end the Kaiser had to be asked to intervene on her behalf. Despite that, the stories continued in the press and although the Kaiser's intercession had some effect it was plain that his position was becoming weakened and the response from the leaders around him was more nominal than sincere.

Early 1915 found Daisy in Bavaria living in a small house in the Alps with her two youngest sons, Lexel and Bolko. Hansel was with Hans completing his formal education and preparing to join the German Army although he was still under-age. However, Daisy and Hans had a short time together in Fürstenstein but it did nothing to repair the tension between them now under-lying their relationship.

It is fair to comment that throughout the war Hans made a great effort to be kind to Daisy in his letters to her while they were apart. His almost paranoiac fear that her presence would not have been tolerated was proved right when the Kaiser invited her to join him at Pless to celebrate her birthday in 1915. Although the Kaiser retained his fondness for her and welcomed her presence, the sentiment was plainly not mirrored by those amongst the senior military who were located at the castle.

Daisy in Red Cross Uniform
Courtesy of Muzeum Zamkowe w Pszczynie, Poland

Hans's letters to Daisy were written in most affectionate tones, using her childhood nickname 'Dany', on occasions sympathising with her position as an English woman living in Germany. He also took her side against the aggression which still continued to be directed at her. Although Daisy appreciated his concern, sadly she could not bring herself to forget the coldness of their relationship in the years which had passed. Daisy was a very warm-hearted person, no doubt through the bloodline of her mother, Patsy, and the Irish streak may have made her the more determined to fight her own cause against the formality which pervaded the German aristocratic families.

During the Summer of 1915, Daisy got a call to work with the Red Cross on a hospital train being run by her old boss at Tempelhof Hospital in Berlin. She took her two sons to Fürstenstein and stayed there while she worked at improving the lot of the injured private soldiers and their families who were in the vicinity, before actually taking up the position on the hospital train in October of that year. That was to be short lived as Professor Kuester was directed that she should not serve on the train and Daisy spent many more months passing her time amongst friends in the country around Fürstenstein.

Efforts to visit Switzerland and Turkey were frustrated by officialdom, and it was not until the Spring of 1916 that Daisy was eventually to get a position to serve on a Lazarett hospital train. She did this until Christmas when she took time off to join the family at Fürstenstein, but in January 1917 she caught pneumonia. This brought on another attack of the circulatory problem which had affected her during the birth of Bolko and as she was unable to return to her work on the hospital train she returned once again to the peace of the Bavarian Alps.

Castle Pless had gradually been taken over as the main military headquarters for Germany and her allies, and was to stay as such until some time in 1917 when the military headquarters was transferred to the Western Front. Daisy was in effect banned from her own home during that period and Hans would not even allow her to stay in the disconnected villa in the grounds. The military leaders were growing more powerful and the influence of the Kaiser was diminishing as the war progressed.

In particular, two of the military leaders Hindenberg and Ludendorff were assuming control over all matters of importance and by August 1916 they achieved their objective of being handed the reins to steer Germany through the war and to its conclusion. In hindsight they did this spectacularly, although not with the result which they perhaps wished to achieve.

July 1917 brought the death, at Newlands Manor, of Daisy's father following an illness. This was just after an unforgettable period at Fürstenstein when Daisy had been advised to keep low and to avoid any publicity or outdoor activity which might provoke demonstrations against her. She had been allowed to stay in a cottage on a remote part of the estate only, not in the main buildings, and with a return of some of her previous ailments had become very depressed.

Later in the year however, things took a turn for the better as she managed to find herself a new position in Belgrade on Red Cross hospital work, which she preceded with a brief and happy holiday with her children. The work was intense and not just among injured soldiers but with their families as well. The year ended with a fairly pleasant family gathering at Berchtesgarten with the children, Hans and Hansel both on leave.

1918 was against Daisy. First came news of her mother, Patsy, being seriously ill, then an old and devoted friend, the Grand Duke Mecklenburg-Strelitz, was found drowned in the grounds of his castle. A most extraordinary and outrageous suggestion in the press followed that he had been Daisy's lover and had also intrigued with her in spying on Germany for England, this matter becoming common gossip in other newspapers. The Kaiser and Hans both stepped in to repudiate the story and Hans took legal steps to challenge the libel, but the matter was settled out of court. Sadly, as the matter was not aired in court with the attendant reporting in the media, Daisy did not get the matter cleared up satisfactorily. This meant that for years her character was tarnished in the minds of those who had never heard the real truth.

The war continued to rage. Hansel sent reports from the Front and Hans took some time off from his duties to be with Daisy in Munich for a rather belated silver wedding celebration. Despite his concern for her during her troubles and the public support he showed for her previous social work, her wartime nursing and hospital service, Daisy did not appear to be able to respond to Hans with affection. The years of differences in their ways of living and previous conflicts had taken their toll. In addition, Daisy had discovered that Hans had been unfaithful to her at an earlier stage of their marriage.

The last year of the war saw Daisy working in hospitals in Serbia and passing some time in Bavaria. Towards the last days of the conflict she left for Austria but just before she left Belgrade she was presented with the Medal Second Class of the Red Cross with War Decoration.

By then the command structure in Germany was collapsing. Britain and her allies were calling for the abdication of the Kaiser as a condition of terms of armistice and unrest amongst working people within Germany was increasing as repressed social feelings rapidly rose to the surface.

Daisy then moved to Munich where she arrived on November 5th just two days before the revolution broke out and the King of Austria fled his country. Led by a mutiny in the German Navy at Kiel the forces of the revolution took over, the Kaiser abdicated and left the country for Holland on November 9th. Princes and dukes were all dispossessed of their power as the German Republic was declared and two days later the war was over.

Unable to return to Fürstenstein, Daisy left Munich for her retreat at Partenkirchen, although even there she found that her house had become a home for a small group of the workers council. Daisy, who had always championed the under classes, however, managed to live there with them in amiable harmony.

POST WAR DAISY

Daisy's war had ended in one sense, but not totally as she could still not get to any of her homes; neither to Fürstenstein to be with Hans and her sons, nor to England to her roots but where the tensions which had arisen over the war years were not calming down with any haste. Her personal war was not to end for some time. Her ability to travel was restricted due to her status of being married to a German and having lived there during the war. It was another sad period in her life.

It was not until the Autumn of 1919 that Daisy eventually was to return to England, and then not even with the usual retinue of servants which had habitually attended her former travels. A lonely journey to London from Southampton was followed by her making her own way through the capital to stay with her old friend Stella Patrick-Campbell, her brother George's wife, although the marriage of these two was not at all happy and they were not living together at the time.

It was not a good visit at all as her mother was still seriously ill. In addition, since her father's death in 1917 all the family estates were either up for sale, as at Ruthin Castle, or, at Newlands Manor, about to be seized by the bailiffs in order to pay off George's debts. Earlier in the year the marriage of her sister Shelagh to the Duke of Westminster had sadly ended in divorce.

Within weeks Daisy left to join Shelagh and Patsy in France where they had a happier time amongst friends, although Daisy first had to obtain special permission to travel. In the Spring of 1920, Daisy then made a trip to Germany to see her family but this was cut short by rushing back to France to help Shelagh take Patsy back home to England before she died.

The rest of the year Daisy was to spend with her sister trying to recover her health, but she then returned to Fürstenstein for a brief time at Christmas. That was unhappy as she and Hans plainly argued about the state of their marriage, and within days she left and went to Baden Baden.

Daisy was now on her own and John Koch quotes from a letter she wrote to King George V in which she asks for his help to assist her, a British subject, so that she did not suffer badly from the result of a divorce.

Curiously, in the Summer of 1921, Daisy officially returned to Fürstenstein, but any hope of a reconciliation was doomed to failure. By the Autumn Daisy was once more back in Partenkirchen. The divorce proceedings dragged on and it was not until December 1923 that it became absolute.

The settlement which Daisy received from Hans was generous; it allowed two residences, one at La Napoule in France on the Riviera coast and the other in a smart part of Munich, together with staff and a vehicle as well as an allowance. Sadly, that was not to be for long as, with the economic climate and the seizure of some Pless property by the new Polish Government, the estate could not afford the outlay. Soon the noose began to tighten on the funds and Daisy was then almost perpetually in financial distress.

The governmental change was brought about by the division of Upper Silesia into two parts, one which remained in Germany, the other being split off to the Polish Republic.

Within Germany, despite the revolution and the discarding of the titled aristocracy from positions of authority, the effect was rather less dramatic, but in Poland no account was taken of former position or previous agreements. Taxes were applied, the same for everyone, to a draconian level.

As a result Hans ultimately had to close down Fürstenstein, which later became a museum, and he moved the family base to Pless. However, this did not happen immediately as it was reported to Daisy that Fürstenstein life had continued at a high level of pomp and with just as many servants, despite the financial state. That all finished in 1925 when the last major event was held in unlimited splendour, the celebration of the wedding of Hans to his new bride Clotilde de Silva; the ceremony having been in London on January 25th.

Later a special Trust was formed to manage the bankrupt mines and other associated industries and this Trust had the task of managing the funds for Daisy, but they were far from generous nor were they prompt in their payments.

Daisy was by now far from fit. She spent much of her time in France whilst the Munich residence was being prepared but the work was slow due to the limit of money available.

When she was not at La Napoule she spent time in various rest homes or sanatoria to assist the problems with her circulation in her legs. Her companion for some time was Ena Fitzpatrick, a cousin on her mother's side of the family, who had also spent the war years in Germany. The two of them were constantly hammering at lawyers representing the Trust in order to get the money due to them.

That partnership came to an end in October 1925 and Daisy's dedicated companion from then on until her death in 1943 was Dolly Crowther. Dolly had looked after Daisy's mother in her illness and was as diligent in looking after her daughter.

Ena Fitzpatrick comes into this story once again with her later involvement with Lexel, Daisy's son, as will be disclosed in a further chapter of this book.

Insofar as Clotilde was concerned, after providing Hans with two daughters and one son who died young, the marriage was to be annulled. Clotilde later married Bolko, Hans and Daisy's son, and they provided a grandson, also called Bolko, for Hans and Daisy. The baby was born in 1936, the same year that his father died.

Daisy was able to move to Munich in 1928 on completion of the work there. Only a few months later she sold La Napoule in France, although she continued to have the benefit of being able to visit from time to time, the last occasion being in the winter of 1932.

Over the next few years there were some very considerable differences of opinion between Hansel and Lexel over management of their mother's affairs, as Lexel was inclined to be less than careful and to exceed the bounds of the authority vested in him by Daisy who had at first made Lexel her attorney. This was solved as Hansel took over the power of attorney and almost shortly afterwards persuaded Daisy to give up the large house at Munich and return to Fürstenstein. She was only able to live in part of the south wing of the gatehouse which had been prepared as an apartment for her and Dolly. So in 1935 Daisy was back where, so many years ago she had commenced her married life, although the castle was by now deserted apart from an inflow of curious visitors.

Daisy continued to suffer from money problems as any payments due from the Pless administration were erratic and there was still a constant battle between the lawyers on the two sides. The truth was that the Pless funds were almost negligible and there was little there to honour their obligations. This unhappy situation continued until a directive was given by the government in some new regulations that as Daisy was a foreigner she was not entitled to any payments at all. With no money coming in, Daisy and Dolly were left to the kind heartedness of the friendly people in the locality for their provisions and minimal necessities.

Hansel, then living in London, pledged a regular sum to her each month. During 1938, the year in which his father died, the visit Hansel made to see Daisy was his last as the war then intervened. In due course, after internment, he served in the British Army, and Lexel served in Polish forces attached to the army. It would be paradoxical for Hansel to fight for Germany in one war and later to serve Britain in another.

Daisy, totally isolated from her family, continued to live at Fürstenstein and then at the behest of her physician she was moved to a very small apartment in the Castle at Waldenberg where she was to live out her remaining life. It was ironic that the English lady was isolated in Europe whilst her two sons, one who had been born German but adopted Polish nationality, were in England or serving with the British forces in the war against Germany.

A few short letters were exchanged between Hansel and Daisy, through the Red Cross in neutral countries, during the early years of the war, until 1943, but it was the devoted Dolly who wrote for the lady who was now totally dependant on her for everything. The once beautiful Daisy was now almost totally paralysed and had to be cared for in every possible way. Some medical records which have been subsequently disclosed indicate that Daisy suffered from the very debilitating Multiple Sclerosis.

In July 1943 Hansel received a letter from Dolly advising him that his mother had died. He later received another letter from his mother's cousin, Countess Olivia Larisch (née Fitzpatrick) which described the last days of her life and the funeral.

Although the Polish authorities had forbidden mass attendance at her funeral, thousands of people from Waldenberg who owed her so much for their improved conditions attended, as did those from Fürstenstein who knew her from happier times. It seems that at the end Daisy had triumphed over adversity.

Her body was buried in the family tomb at Fürstenstein. Daisy had always said that she did not want to be buried there. At the end of the war the tomb was stripped by vandals for valuables. The local people took her body and re-buried it where she had always wanted, amongst the trees and flowers of the local fields.

The light-hearted Daisy, who had lived through times which took her from the highest places of state to the poverty and illness of her latter years, finally rested in peace.

One of the strangest factors about Princess Daisy's life was that although her marriage was not happy and ended with divorce, she continued to live in Germany or other neighbouring countries right until her death. At the start of the First World War, when she was visiting England and perhaps could have been excused for remaining there, she really put herself out to get back to Fürstenstein.

After the war she basically remained on the continent, apart from the occasional journeys, but even those were inhibited by her frailty. She could have decided to break away and return to England to live amongst her birth family and friends, but even with her eldest son Hansel then living so much of his time in England she chose not to do so. We shall never know why.

THE LOVES OF HER LIFE

Firstly let it be said that there is no evidence that Daisy was ever other than truly faithful to her husband Hans. However, there will be few couples who in their lives have not experienced some pull of friendship with the opposite sex which, if left uncontrolled, would affect the main marital relationship.

In that respect, the 19th century would be no different from the 20th and 21st centuries, despite any veneer of respectability, although modern tolerances are perhaps rather more malleable than in earlier times.

Apart from the possibility of any childhood crushes, which even in Victorian times would be the case as the young ladies met interesting young men, Daisy was known to be very much attached to one young aristocrat, an officer in the army. Mysteriously at about the time of her introduction to Hans the young man was posted abroad to one of the areas of conflict at the time, and he did not return. It has been suggested that this was preparatory work done by Patsy who was looking much further afield for a match with high position and money.

It has already been recorded how at the start of her marriage to Hans she had no romantic feelings towards him, but that she hoped these would emerge as time progressed. It was a struggle which was never to be settled, as often when one of them showed affection the other stood off.

Some three years into her marriage, at the time when she was trying to resolve her relationship with her husband Hans, Daisy had developed a friendship with a young man. 'Gordy' is the name which is mentioned in her diaries, and it seems he may have been Gordon Woods, but although there was a great deal of fondness between them that was where it stayed. There is no indication of any other involvement, and it must have been that the friendship gave her some support to endure the rather formal attitudes within her marriage.

It started at a time when Daisy and Hans were visiting England through the period 1894-95 when there were many social events and Gordy was ever present. At times when Hans was being entertained elsewhere, Gordy accompanied Daisy. He followed her around and was plainly infatuated with her, but when the gossips began to talk about the friendship he was perhaps the one who became the most upset.

So far as Daisy was concerned, here was a young man paying her attention at a time when she was struggling to come to terms with her marriage, when her husband was so unemotional and when she was still childless. Gordy was a confidante and a companion and there is no doubt that Daisy had strong feelings for him.

He undoubtedly filled a part of her life from which true love was being excluded at a time when her own natural passions were at their height. But Daisy left him in England and returned to Germany with her husband.

To a lesser extent another friendship with a George Cooper enters Daisy's diaries, but that too was left unrequited.

Both Gordy and George died, and whatever emotion had been attached to their friendship died with them.

It was not to be the last time that Daisy became emotionally involved with another, as is related in Koch's biography of Daisy and supported by comments in her copious diaries; but as with the first friendship, however intense the feelings were between the parties, it was no more than that.

This romantic interlude which came into Daisy's life involved a suitor who was probably from the Hapsburg monarchy. The identity of the person is not disclosed in any of Daisy's diaries and Koch in his book keeps the secret.

The man she named as Maxl first came on the scene in 1899 and that singular but deep and rewarding friendship lasted until 1910 in this form when he married.

The tone of the correspondence indicated that this was a very passionate affair but only in correspondence and words, there being absolutely no evidence from the diaries or in any other way that any more physical passions had ever engaged the two correspondents. In due course when Maxl married, both he and his wife retained very friendly contact with Daisy and visited each other. A final meeting between the two took place in 1913 at Pless when Maxl and his wife visited Daisy.

It can be seen from this interlude and the earlier approaches from Gordy that Daisy, although still uncomfortable in the marital relationship with her husband, was loyal to him and for long enough tried her best to make the marriage work. Undoubtedly these other relationships gave some outlet for her subsumed passions but it seems certain that such were kept under control and never ventured beyond the written or spoken word.

However, those readers who wish to follow the detail of these passionate interludes in Daisy's life must of course obtain copies of her diaries and read for themselves, and then make up their own minds as to the strength of feelings between the parties, and the part they played in Daisy's life.

A conclusion which can be reached from this summary of Daisy's life is that she was a talented and passionate lady. Although she undoubtedly suffered from what would these days be classified as a form of depression over her unfulfilled marriage, she overcame that. Her talents helped her to succeed as a hostess as well as in that other sphere of social work which became an important part of her life. The illness which afflicted her came at quite an early age when she gave birth to her third son, Bolko, and it was to affect her life from then on.

Her final years of illness and poor circumstances could only have been made bearable by the devotion of her companion, Dolly. It is a sad postscript that after Daisy's death, when Dolly was trying to escape to the West with a companion, they were overtaken by the advancing Russian forces and were killed.

Whereas those in Europe who sought the overturning of the ruling classes in favour of the workers would not have shed a tear on Princess Daisy's behalf, she had earned a place in the hearts of the many who knew her for her kindness, and her life is a sad and very human story.

TWELVE
DUCHESS SHELAGH

The youngest of the children from the marriage of William and Patsy was born on 15th February 1878. She was christened Constance Edwina but, as with the rest of the family, she soon acquired a familiar name. This was Shelagh, the spelling of which firmly associated her with her Irish mother.

Her childhood, which was shared with siblings George and Daisy, suffered from the same distant motherhood from Patsy and the benign tolerance of William. Shelagh enjoyed the many delights of the Newlands estate in the South but her special fondness was for Ruthin and the pleasures of the neighbouring estate of Eaton, near Chester, a mere twenty miles away as the crow flies, where the Grosvenor family lived in considerable splendour.

Why, might one ask, was this neighbouring estate so popular? It was due to the young man, Hugh Richard Arthur Grosvenor, who was living there. He was as a child, the direct heir to the Dukedom of Westminster and he eventually took this title in succession as the 2nd Duke directly from his grandfather, as his own father had died some years before.

The Duke's nickname Bend'Or was derived from the name of a racehorse owned by his grandfather that had won the Derby in 1880, which in turn had been based on a historical matter relating to the family coat of arms.

Although all of the children from the two families played and mixed together, Shelagh and Bend'Or were to fall for each other in childhood and that led to marriage on 18th February 1901 shortly after he returned home from serving in the South African Boer war. They had many common interests, one being a love of horses and riding, another was yachting. They both had a passion for racing cars, which was then a relatively new form of pastime.

Shelagh had been endowed with the good looks of the rest of her family, both parents exceeding in this department, with her sister Daisy being a noted beauty, and her brother George a very handsome fellow.

As a hostess, Shelagh was very able, taking on the task at the family seat of Eaton in Cheshire as well as at the magnificent town house in London, Grosvenor House. Entertaining there was on a very grand scale and hosting such events must have been a considerable task for such an inexperienced wife, but it seems that she acquitted herself very well.

Her marriage to the Duke was very much a love match and started out well but unhappily it did not turn out to be lasting as the relationship between the two young lovers became weakened by a sequence of events.

Shelagh and her sister Daisy, although quite different in their character, were very close and during the unhappy years of Daisy's marriage, Shelagh spent a lot of time with her in Germany, as well as accompanying her on her travels. Long absences from Bend'Or must have affected their marriage and unhappy circumstances surrounding their children were to be the breaking point.

Their first child, Ursula, was born in 1902. This beautiful young lady was to develop a lifelong and very supportive friendship with Hansel, her cousin by her aunt Daisy.

Eaton Hall
The Duke of Westminster's family seat

The next child, born in 1904, was Edward George Hugh but sadly his life was to be short as he died from an illness when he was five, depriving the Duke of his first heir. Unfortunately this appears to have been when his mother was on one of her visits to see Daisy. The circumstances of his death are related by George Ridley in his book about Bend'Or that the boy took ill with a temperature, wrongly diagnosed as a minor stomach problem at first. Later it was found to be appendicitis yet even then a few more days were to elapse before an operation was carried out at Eaton Hall. By then septicaemia had set in and within another week the young child died.

From then on, their relationship which had been drifting for some time took a turn for the worse. Although the marriage had been one based on love its smooth course had not been helped from the start by the rather extreme lifestyles of the Cornwallis-Wests, especially Patsy who was an avowed follower of the Prince of Wales and others in the rather fast Edwardian set, which compared rather unfavourably with the more traditional nature of the Grosvenor family.

The propensity of the Cornwallis-Wests to go through money at speed was not one with which the Duke had much sympathy. Although not at all mean, he was a careful man in such matters. The variety of appeals which were made by William to support the family loans and then some later efforts made to assist young George in his wayward financial ways became tiresome.

A third child was conceived and there was hope for a boy to replace the lost heir, but sadly that was not to be. The child, Mary, was born in June 1910 and it is remarked that the Duke did not even bother to see the new child once he knew it was not a boy.

The marriage struggled on until 1913 when the Duke asked for a separation which Shelagh declined. The First World War intervened and the Duke went off to battle, earning considerable credit for his actions. Shelagh, like her sister Daisy, took to looking after wounded soldiers and she opened a hospital at Le Touquet in France, later being awarded the CBE for her loyal service and dedication to the task.

It is interesting that the two sisters were doing the same work, although in Daisy's case she was looking after the German soldiers on the opposite side of the war.

The Duke's adultery then gave Shelagh the opportunity to sue for divorce and that came about in 1917.

In 1920, Shelagh married again, this time to an airman, Wing Commander James Fitzpatrick Lewes. They set up their new home at Lyndhurst in the New Forest, not many miles away from her one time childhood home at Newlands, and there they became widely known for their love of country pursuits. Her second husband died in 1965.

Shelagh lived to a considerable age, being 92 when she died in 1970. In an interesting follow up to the support she had given her sister around the earlier war years when her marriage was in disarray, Shelagh turned her hand to helping Daisy's son, Hansel, when he was interned in England during the Second World War, and her daughter Ursula was a very close confidante and friend to Hansel throughout his life. Ursula's first marriage to William Filmer-Sankey was dissolved in 1940, and in the same year she married a Major Stephen Vernon.

This book will not pursue the extension of Shelagh's family connections.

Her first husband, the 2nd Duke of Westminster married three more times but had no male issue, so on his death in 1953 the titles passed to a cousin, William.

THE NEXT GENERATIONS

William Cornwallis Cornwallis-West m Mary Adelaide Virginia Thomasina Eupatoria Fitzpatrick
1835-1917   m 1872   1855-1920

George Frederick Myddleton	Mary Theresa Olivia	** Constance Edwina
(George)	(Daisy)	(Shelagh)
1874 -1951	1873-1943	1878-1970
Jennie Churchill	Hans 3rd Prince of Pless	2nd Duke of Westminster
m 1900 div 1914	m 1891 div 1923	m1901 div1917
Stella Patrick Campbell		Ursula b 21.2.1902
m1914 div1940		m(1)1924 (2)1940
Georgette Hirsch		Edward 1904-09
m 1940-1951		Mary 27.6.1910
No Issue		** see below

Clotilde *m 1925 ann 1934

Hans	Alexander	Bolko m 1934		
1900-1984	1905-1984	1910-1936		Konrad b 1930 d 1934
m(1) 1924	No issue			
Sissy		(2daughters)		
Div 1952		Bolko 6th Prince of Pless		
m(2) 1958		b1936-		
Mary				
Div 1970		m 1964 div 1969		
No issue		1 Daughter b 1965		

* Clotilde de Silva y Gonzales de Candamo
  of the Spanish House of the Marques de Arcicollar

** Neither the extension of the family of Shelagh and The Duke of Westminster, nor that of her second marriage are included here, as their stories are not being related in this book.

THE HOCHBERG (PLESS) FAMILY

Although Daisy's husband has been mentioned in Chapter 11, before continuing with the rest of this story it will be useful to explain some background to the family.

The origins go back to the thirteenth century at least, and it is noted by John Koch in his biography of Daisy that in 1292 a Polish Duke from Schweidner-Jauer, who was also a member of the Piast dynasty, rulers of the Kingdom of Poland, became the owner of Castle Fürstenstein in Silesia. Later in 1509, the Hochberg family acquired the castle and from then on developed it in size and quality, major improvements happening during the 18th century.

The family benefited from the huge mineral deposits in the area, especially the mines which produced an enormous quantity of coal. This expansion of wealth, which brought in towns and villages as well as huge areas of agricultural land, was given a boost in 1847 when the head of the family succeeded to the title of Fürst von Pless, or Prince of the Principality of Pless in Upper Silesia, then a part of Germany. The area owned by the family therefore covered part of Poland as well as Germany and, as can be imagined, this was to be the cause of much tension and international wrangling in the coming years. The family was quite possibly the richest in Germany and Poland.

The male family titles are Graf von Hochberg, Freiherr zu Fürstenstein.

This Fürst von Pless in 1847 was Hans Heinrich X, whose son Hans Heinrich XI was to be the father-in-law, great friend and comfort to Daisy in her marriage to his son Hans Heinrich XV, and who helped her in the social work she undertook. '*Vater*', as she called him, was the 'rock' to whom she could turn in the earlier years of her marriage, until his death in August 1907.

Daisy's husband, Hans Heinrich XV, fathered three sons by her: Hansel born in 1900, Lexel in 1905 and Bolko in 1910 and a fourth son Konrad was born of his second marriage to Clotilde de Silva.

This marriage to Clotilde was annulled in 1934. Clotilde married her ex-husband's third son Bolko. An heir, Bolko Constantin, was born in 1936. He is known as Bolko Graf von Hochberg und Fürst von Pless, and is living in Munich.

Other branches of the Hochberg family have been prolific.

Castle Pless

Castle Fürstenstein

Both Pictures by courtesy of W. John Koch

THE LATER GENERATIONS

HANS HEINRICH
(HANSEL)

Courtesy of Muzeum Zamkowe w Pszczynie, Poland

ALEXANDER FREDERICK
(LEXEL)

BOLKO CONRAD
(BOLKO)

Both Pictures by Courtesy of W. John Koch

THIRTEEN
HANSEL

Hans Heinrich William Albert Edward was born in Berlin on 2nd February 1900. His father was Hans and his mother was Daisy. In due course the baby, thereafter to be known as Hansel, was to succeed to the titles then held by his grandfather and afterwards by his father, as His Serene Highness Hans Heinrich XVII, Prince of Pless. The two regal Christian names William and Edward indicated the support of his godfathers the Emperor of Germany and the Prince of Wales, the future King of England.

There can not have been a more auspicious and well provided start to life for any child. His father's family had the ownership of three large castles in Silesia and his mother's family at the time held two notable country houses, Ruthin Castle in Wales and Newlands Manor in Hampshire. The Pless family was one of the richest, even possibly the richest in Germany.

When he died eighty four years later, although still nominally the holder of all the titles, it was to be his preference to be known as Mr Henry Pless. The castles and houses had all gone, together with the wealth, and he was living in extremely modest circumstances in England. He had no male family from his marriages, so the titles then moved sideways to his brother who died one month later.

The intervening period of his life was to take him through one world war where he fought for his father's country and a second conflict which saw him first imprisoned in England as an alien but then he was later released to serve for a while in the forces of his mother's homeland. Thereafter, for the rest of his life he lived in England in very reduced circumstances.

Hansel's life is well documented in a book by Michael Luke, *Hansel Pless - Prisoner of History*, and if readers who are stimulated by the following narrative wish to learn more, they would be well advised and recommended to obtain a copy.

From a young age, Hansel was groomed by his father for the position he was intended to inherit, being the eldest son in the family and therefore as such the heir to the property and the titles. This made a big distinction between him and his younger brothers who were to be left far more to the care of their mother.

Towards the outbreak of the First World War, although being too young to serve in the army, he was nevertheless sent by his father to be trained in his regiment. In due course he was to serve both on the Eastern Front against the Russians, then on the Western Front against the French, British and Americans. In the process he was awarded the Iron Cross, First Class.

Such are the peculiarities of war, and with his background of parents from two different countries he even came across a relation amongst the British prisoners of war and took the time to speak to him. It must have been a very strange experience indeed to be fighting on the one side with a mother who came from the enemy country.

After that war he spent the next few years learning about the family investments and their industrial background and was appointed to a position in the organisation.

Despite being placed in charge of a considerable part of the family businesses, Hansel then spent many of the years between the two wars living a great deal of the time in England and travelling to Germany and Poland as necessary for business purposes. Later, he, his father and brothers were to take Polish nationality and it was as such that Hansel eventually became a resident in England. He later received British nationality not, however, without first being made to serve three years confinement as an alien during the early part of the Second World War. This was despite the fact that at the time he held the nationality of the very country for which Britain had entered the war, Poland.

One purpose of this re-orientation of nationality by the family was to try to mitigate the strong attitude being taken by the Polish government in the matter of taxes and their attempts to control the Pless enterprises.

After the eventful years of the First World War, with the abdication of the Emperor Wilhelm and the German revolution which demoted the titled people from places of high office, the life of the Pless family changed.

Before Hansel was demobilised in 1919, he was involved in policing actions to try to quell the worst aspects of the revolution. Immediately afterwards on his return to Fürstenstein and Pless he helped to mobilise the staff and workers on the estates to resist an attempt by the Communists to take over the business and properties. The family were successful and it was resolved without any conflict.

Then Hansel attempted to return to the more normal life of being a student in Berlin at the Friedrich Wilhelm University, where he studied law, history and economics. He was to need all of these skills, especially the legal one in his future life. His time at university was comfortable as his parents had many friends there from their many years of social life with the Kaiser and the Court in much happier times. However, Hansel did not prove to be a particularly sociable character especially in the rather frenetic life of post-war Berlin, preferring more serious connections amongst the diplomats with whom he came into contact. He eventually obtained a doctorate.

As his father's heir, Hansel suffered the problems which arose as the Polish and German authorities fought over the many Pless industrial interests. Curiously it was to be the defeated Germans who provided the support for the family against the grasping hand of the

Polish state. These struggles were to continue right up to and through the Second World War until the Polish government, then under the controlling hand of Moscow, nationalised the industries in 1946. In those intervening years the problem of Silesia's position: half German, half Polish and for years under the influence of the Tsar before the German forces took control after the Russian revolution, then losing it again with the Armistice, was to continue.

An aggravation to the post 1914-18 war situation was French obduracy, particularly in respect of the Silesian question, and their requirement of the removal of the industrial and mineral deposits from any form of German control, despite the predominance of the region's population having German nationality and the wish of a plebiscite amongst the residents to remain associated with that country. The matter rumbled on with Lloyd George in England taking a very keen interest in the affair.

At one time, some Polish insurgents with the tacit support of the French attempted to seize assets by force. The British responded with the despatch of troops to the country. Aided by local volunteers including Hansel with a unit from Fürstenstein, the insurgents were defeated.

Despite that, in 1921 the League of Nations ruled that Silesia should be divided up, irrespective of the nationality of its residents. Thus some Germans ended up living in Poland and vice versa and even some industrial areas were broken into illogical separate units.

These post war machinations were to be the hard rock of family life within the Pless family over the years. It was not just the authorities whom Hansel had to fight. His own brother Lexel proved to be a considerable difficulty, and in the latter years of their father's life especially, the plotting and manoeuvrings against Hansel were considerable.

It was in 1922 that Hansel, Lexel and their father Hans all took Polish nationality because of the way the state had been divided, at the same time declaring that Pless would become the main family residence, albeit that Fürstenstein remained the favourite property where Hans lived most of the time.

Hans at first tried to ride out the years after the First World War when inflation set in, as the family finances were supported by investments which had been made in Switzerland, but gradually realism took over and by half way through the 1920s the rot set in; rooms had to be closed off and the social life seriously curtailed. However, that was not before there were some final celebrations at Fürstenstein to mark Hansel's university successes and after his wedding in Dresden to Sissy on 4th December 1924.

Hansel first met Sissy when he was only fifteen years of age and he was smitten by her. A member of the family von Schonborn-Wiesentheid, she was christened Maria and was first to be married to another, give birth to a son and be divorced before she married Hansel some nine years later.

Then, Hansel's father, after his divorce from Daisy and an elopement to London for a marriage ceremony to his new young bride Clotilde in 1925, marked the occasion with a considerable function at Fürstenstein. That was really to be the last of the extravagant events and quite shortly afterwards reductions were made in staff and the castle was half closed down. Eventually it became more of a museum and tourist attraction than a home.

About this time there was concern in the family about Lexel and his proclivities to be attracted to young men, and for which he received a prison sentence as homosexuality was illegal. Clotilde was quite firmly against Lexel being around her and he was banished with a tutor to tour countries in the Middle East. Eventually he went to France and then to Munich and for some time lived with his mother, Daisy.

Further complications arose as Bolko and Clotilde carried on a relationship behind Hans's back; eventually this led to the annulment of the marriage, with Clotilde and Bolko departing the scene to get married and raise their own children.

Through all these upheavals Hansel showed a calm front and he did what he could to assist his father in matters of the companies and the estates as their own claims, and counter claims by the Polish authorities, rumbled on through the courts.

It was during this period, from the mid 1920s until 1933, when Germany left the League of Nations that the Pless family had to rely on the German state to support them against the demands of the Poles, which were ruining the companies financially. Germany was compliant in that respect as they also wished to prevent the Poles taking over more and more of Silesia. They provided funds behind the scenes to assist the task of keeping the 30,000 or so Pless employees off the breadline as the Poles were trying to almost starve the companies into giving up their fight against Polish domination.

The deliberations and activities of these times kept Hansel well occupied whether he was in London or Germany. It should also be noted that the Poles were in breach of an order by the International Court of Justice in The Hague and received a reprimand for their activities. However, it did not prevent them from committing Hansel to prison for employing an alien citizen, from Danzig.

Hansel was not at ease with life in Germany, nor Poland, and he had far more affinity with his mother's birth country, England. As has already been noted he decided that he should live permanently in England and did his best to persuade Sissy to accompany him but she would not go. They did not have any children but she had a young son from her first marriage. Although not an ardent Nazi, she was more comfortable with the resurgence of German nationalism which had by then arisen under Hitler's hand and she remained in her native land.

So, in 1933 Hansel left for England and took accommodation in London. He found a place in Little Stanhope Street where he installed himself with a small staff. To assist him in his management of the family businesses in Europe he engaged a personal secretary.

In the years after 1933, Sissy and Hansel met when he visited Poland or Germany, but they were not very happy occasions. However, the correspondence between them tended to be couched in friendlier terms, so there must have remained some softer feelings.

In the early days of the National Socialist uprising, Hansel's brothers Lexel and Bolko at first aligned themselves to the cause of the Nazi movement and this was the cause of a deal of discomfort between them and Hansel. However, the Nazi enthusiasm of the two brothers was to be short lived and in due course Lexel was to serve with the Polish forces in support of Britain in the 1939-45 War.

This period during the early 1930s brought a great deal of unhappiness and problems for Hansel. He saw Sissy only occasionally and his two brothers were conspiring against him and their father, Hans. Lexel engaged in some rather duplicitous dealings with the German and Polish authorities, as did Bolko, but in addition the latter made efforts to blackmail his father to pay off his considerable debts.

There would seem to be little doubt that the two younger brothers had been somewhat cushioned from the harsh realities of the 1914-18 War by living much of the time with their mother. Hansel had been under his father's wing until he joined up, so the influence of the male adult with the firm discipline from years of seriously responsible Teutonic family background must have had an effect on the young officer.

Despite being one with equally long ancestral ties through the De La Warr line, Daisy's family had been worldlier and much more engaged in the very light-hearted frivolities of Edwardian England. Her general attitude to life was more relaxed following her own free and easy upbringing. This must have given the two younger sons a far broader outlook and possibly a less responsible attitude as they spent so much time with her, although that would have been no reason for them to indulge later in dishonesty and family intrigue against their brother and father.

As described in Michael Luke's book about Hansel, it seems that the two younger brothers conspired together and with other agencies to have Hansel removed from his authoritative position in the Pless organisation, and for Lexel to be put in place instead.

In addition, as the result of considerable misrepresentation, a warrant was put out to arrest Hansel for supposed acts of perjury, amongst other matters. Although they were successful in their aim to an extent that for a period Hansel lost the singular control he had exercised since his father had vested that in him in 1925, the tussle continued for many years, causing considerable grief to their father, Hans, whose health was deteriorating badly. When he died in 1938, his direct heir, Hansel, once again came to the fore as the head of the family and its industries and estates, but the struggles continued. However, Bolko had died in 1936 and that left only Lexel to carry on the campaign against Hansel.

Hansel, in the meantime was seeking to get British nationality and his application was supported by no less than his uncle the Duke of Westminster, who happened to be a rather close friend of Winston Churchill. Sadly he was not to get that privilege until much later, and that would only be after he, who was the most British in attitude of the three brothers, had served three years as an alien in confinement during the Second World War, this also despite his nationality being Polish.

The war started in 1939 but his arrest under the Defence Regulation 18B was not to take place until August 1940, after he had made a number of fruitless attempts to join up in the forces or into one of the home defence organisations, but had not been accepted. The Regulation allowed a grossly draconian act of holding citizens in custody without trial, and who then could be kept in such custody at the whim of the Home Secretary without ever being brought before a court of justice.

This unsatisfactory state of affairs held people on remand. As they had not been tried and convicted of any offence, they could not be held in full custody. The dividing line was very marginal, the only difference being that a remand permitted detainees to wear their own clothes and they had a wider opportunity to receive visitors, but not much else other than a little more freedom within the precincts of the prison.

The so-called aliens were swept up in this catch-all process, and there was little or no distinction between any who might really be a problem and others who were merely in the country by force of circumstances, as workers in the hospitality business, such as foreign chefs or others in service. Even the hapless ones who might have fled from oppression on the continent could have been held.

Hansel had two points against him, his birth in Berlin and his service in the First World War in the German Army. The credits on his side were considerable: an English mother, a King of England as godfather and an uncle who was a leading English peer. He was a naturalised Pole, his childhood had been spent almost as much in England as in Germany or Poland and since 1932 he had lived almost constantly in England. He was seeking British nationality and had offered his services to the armed forces of the Crown. But it made no difference. Into the sin bin he went!

Not unreasonably Hansel felt extremely upset at this sudden hand of the State on his shoulder, and he was even less happy when he was moved in very short order to Walton Gaol in Liverpool, a place not greatly noted for the quality of its living conditions. The move was made slightly less unfortunate though as it brought him within range of Eaton Hall, the seat of the Duke of Westminster in Cheshire, and within visiting distance of his devoted cousin Ursula Grosvenor, although by then she had changed her name through marriage and was about to do so once again following a divorce.

Ursula was the only visitor Hansel received whilst at Walton, but he later gathered in the support of his uncle, George Cornwallis-West and his aunt, Shelagh, the 2nd Duchess of Westminster.

Hansel was to stay at Walton until later in 1940 when he was transferred to a camp at Ascot and it was there he waited his turn to be brought before the special Advisory Committee who would hear his application to be released.

In summary, the grounds which were given for his detention were: that he was German by birth, well disposed towards the Nazi regime, anti-Polish in his attitude, (no doubt because of his tussles with the Polish authorities over the family businesses), his wife supported the Nazi regime, his business interests would benefit from a German victory, he had been in touch with his wife in Germany since the war began, had actively opposed the war against Germany, he could be easily pressurised by German influence on his wife and mother and that the German government specifically approved his presence in England.

Hansel's legal training enabled him to look closely at these allegations and to prepare logical responses to each one, all of which he denied. The grounds on which MI5 had made them were not particularly easy to ascertain, but Hansel worked hard to set out his stall to make his case as thoroughly as he was able. Time dragged on so it was not until December that he was to appear before the tribunal, headed by an extremely eminent judge, Norman Birkett KC.

Unfortunately, as Hansel was unaware of the basis on which some of the allegations had been made against him, he was unable to refute them strongly enough to persuade the tribunal of how invalid they were. Despite the calm and deliberate method of the Advisory Committee, as the tribunal was named, and the careful non-aggressive nature of the proceedings, Hansel failed to convince them of his innocence.

In the summary of their findings they did not specifically support any of the accusations, but decided in more general terms. They considered that with his very wide connections amongst the German authorities he could genuinely be open to being manipulated, and they were unconvinced of his total loyalty to the country of his mother's birth, England. They were sceptical about his efforts to volunteer to serve in the armed forces and seemed to find his very meticulous manner a cause for some concern. On balance, although they could not specifically find any one of the several allegations proved, indeed they made that point in their summary, they had to be extremely cautious in the interests of Britain and therefore felt that the detention should continue.

Hansel was completely thrown by their decision, which he did not receive until March 1941 and heard via the Home Secretary. By then he had once again been moved, this time from Ascot to Huyton Detention Camp which was near Liverpool. Although he responded at once to that Minister it was to no avail; he received no further explanation.

In the latter part of 1941 he was again moved, this time to a camp on the Isle of Man. It was here that Hansel set out in earnest to obtain his release from what was now becoming a very irksome incarceration. Restrictions in the physical sense were not particularly onerous, but the mental effect was debilitating, as people of all types and attitudes were held together within the camp boundary. Although not by nature an anti-social person, Hansel found some of his prison companions not to his taste, especially those who were in support of the very extreme views of Moseley.

Somehow he got hold of a typewriter and he set about his aim of getting his freedom, with considerable vigour. Not just his Uncle Bennie, The Duke of Westminster, but several others whom he knew or perhaps had been introduced to in his social life were to receive many letters in this personal war against his detention. In addition, those politicians who had expressed concerns about the draconian powers of the Defence Regulation Act in Parliament were at the receiving end of his correspondence, and some took the trouble to respond to him expressing their sympathy. However, the hard line Home Secretary, Herbert Morrison, was unmoved.

Hansel was to remain in the Isle of Man, but early in 1942 he was again interviewed by an intelligence officer at the camp, and as a direct result he was sent back to the mainland to be held at Brixton prison in London. Because of the rule by the governor, the conditions were equable and gave Hansel the time and facilities to continue his attempt to get his release. He was greatly supported by Ursula, Shelagh and George, all from the Cornwallis-West line.

Hansel received a visit from his solicitor to enquire how he was proceeding with the representations he wished to make to the Advisory Committee and there were developments from that when the committee set up another hearing which took place between June and July 1942. The detail of this hearing is neatly reported in Michael Luke's book but to paraphrase the position would be to say that the tribunal took a new line in their deliberations. They seemed to dwell more on the positive side than on the negatives. Their conclusion was that they felt the order against Hansel could be suspended with safety, providing that measures were put in place to restrain his movements.

This report was forwarded to the Home Secretary. Despite its favourable opinion, after reading the report, he decided not to act on the recommendations and declared in October 1942 that the order would not be suspended. George Cornwallis-West tried to persuade him otherwise but to no avail. Even when questions were raised later in Parliament on this specific case by Winston Churchill himself,

Home Secretary Morrison remained unmoved. However, it did seem that he might be feeling irked that so many people in influential positions were pressurising for the release of Hansel.

Another rather curious matter then stirred some muddy water and this was to involve the notable family of Londonderry. The son of the Countess, Lord Castlereagh, remarked at an afternoon tea in the presence of Shelagh Duchess of Westminster, that another lady, Muriel Lowther, had made a statement about having visited Hansel in Huyton Gaol when he had confessed to spying for Germany. This was indeed a libel as the lady in question had never visited Hansel at Huyton, a fact which could be proved quite simply from the records of the prison. Thus, the scene was set for a libel action to take place against Castlereagh.

The matter was further compounded by a letter Castlereagh then wrote to George-Cornwallis West which caused Hansel, via his solicitor, to set about bringing an additional case for slander. The matter ploughed its way through the preliminaries for consideration of being settled out of court, and in due course a letter was received from the solicitors for Castlereagh offering an apology, although this was couched in terms which made it plain that the apology was regarded as being quite unnecessary and that the giver was being magnanimous.

These events all took place in 1943, in the same year of Hansel's mother's death in April, only a day after her 70th birthday, and were to continue right through the Summer until the Autumn.

It was in September of 1943 that Hansel Pless was suddenly advised that he was to be released, his order having been revoked. Within hours he was out of Brixton and taking shelter in his Aunt Shelagh's London home. Just a few days later he was drafted into the Royal Army Service Corps, in which he served throughout the rest of the war, rising to the rank of lieutenant.

The word 'revoke' is significant in that it specifically implies that the order which had been placed on him should never have been made in the first place.

What had brought about that change, after the Home Secretary had three times confirmed the order, will always be questioned as it is not on any known record how or why it had been revoked. Is it possible that the case against Castlereagh had lifted the lid on some unsavoury dealings in the security services? One should ask how or why, at some time, had that noble seemingly obtained a copy of MI5 secret documents relating to Hansel's case, which he then used to suggest that Hansel was a risk to Britain's security.

It is all the more curious that Lexel, the brother who really had Nazi sympathies at one time, had subsequently enlisted in the Polish Army and was garrisoned in Scotland, and had been allowed to serve with them in various theatres of war. The only difference in Lexel's case was that he had been born in London, yet of the same English mother and German father.

When the war ended in 1945 Hansel applied to remain in the army, at least for a while, as he had no job, no money to speak of and no home to go to.

That state of affairs only lasted for a short while and in July of the next year Hansel was discharged from the army. Just under a year later, in May 1946, he finally received his naturalisation papers which turned him into a British subject.

In respect of his business affairs, in January 1946 the Pless mines in Lower Silesia were nationalised and some intense legal struggles then took place between Hansel and Lexel's different interests. Already prior to the end of the war Lexel had been trying to get the Germans to buy Fürstenstein but that all fell through. After the war Lexel tried to assign parts of the companies to new holding cover companies in the USA and in Britain.

At the end of the war, Hansel was helped by his wife Sissy who had gone to Pless in order to represent his interests, this despite the rather wide gulf which had arisen between them during the long war years.

Lexel's behaviour had resulted in him being excluded from Daisy's will, so Hansel was the sole beneficiary but any chance to sort out the family affairs was aborted by the complexity of the situation which had arisen, not just within the family but also due to the long running battle between German and Polish national interests. It seemed that the best Hansel could hope for would be his share of reparation money, and he eventually did start to receive that.

As for the castles, Fürstenstein was ravaged by the Russians and such of the fittings which had not been sold off by Lexel were looted or ruined in the aftermath of the war. Waldenberg continued to be in the hands of the local authority, so there was no value there. Pless was acquired by the state but thankfully was not destroyed by the victorious armies. In recent times this has really been the best museum recording the lives and times of the former Princes of Pless, although improvements to Fürstenstein have now brought that to the fore as a notable museum of those earlier times.

Some of Daisy's jewellery had been pawned by Lexel and the rest, including the famous Pless pearls vanished in some military vehicle, although later it was commented that apparently some had been seen adorning Ena Fitzpatrick after she had taken up with Lexel.

Hansel did not benefit. He continued to live a solitary life in a small bed sitter near the Kings Road in London which he rented from some time in 1947. Any financial support probably came from his uncle and cousins in the Westminster family.

Hansel and Sissy eventually agreed to divorce. Although they had remained emotionally attached and addressed each other in the most endearing terms, Hansel had been very upset that Sissy had not felt she could move to England with him before the war and this soured the relationship, at least insofar as he was concerned. However, it was not until May 1952, after much heartrending correspondence and meetings, that the divorce was made absolute. Although Hansel in due course found happiness elsewhere, Sissy remained faithful to the memory of the one she had fallen in love with so many years ago as a teenager, and never married again.

Half a century had passed since Hansel had entered the world and the greater part of that had either been passed in the luxury of the family into which he was born or in the dismal days of war. Now he had to find a life and a way to keep his body and soul together. The first thing he did was to rid himself of the trappings of his former status and power by calling himself Mr Henry Pless.

For relaxation he went up to Cheshire where his uncle Bennie lived at Eaton Hall, and he took long walks in the country. He had acquired a bicycle, nick-named 'The Green Steed', on which he rode many miles, indeed it is said all the way up to Cheshire from London, and later on he purchased a small motor-cycle. This kept him in contact with his Grosvenor cousins who had been so much help to him during the war years, especially during his confinement.

He then set about a business venture which had been in his mind for some time, ever since he had been touring the Eaton estates with his uncle who grumbled at the time wasted to season timber after it had been felled. Hansel had looked into a process for the preservation of timber by using what he referred to as 'electronics'. At the end of the war he had been granted a posting, during his extension period, in order to be near an industrial chemist; so perhaps we can assume that this was for the purpose of investigating his process, for which he then obtained a provisional patent.

He set up a small factory in Norfolk, supported by Bend'Or and with a small staff, but this must surely have also been paid for by him as Hansel's finances were not at all good, indeed at times they were dire. Michael Luke refers to the fact that at one time Hansel had to live in a glorified garden shed in Clapham, but even when properly housed his circumstances remained modest.

Things took a difficult turn for him when the Duke died in 1953 as there was no specific provision in his will for Hansel. The family rectified this omission later, in 1957, but for the time it bore heavily on Hansel who took himself off to Paris where he tried to make some progress with the affairs of his family estate. He made little advancement and returned to London to the dubious pleasure of a bed-sitter.

One of his neighbours was a young lady, Mary Minchin, who had been introduced to him and they commenced to see each other. After some period of courting they were married on 23rd July 1958. They lived in the small house which had by then been gifted to Hansel by the Grosvenors, and managed a pleasant life with a few visits abroad in the course of which it is said that they occasionally stayed with Lexel and Ena in France.

It seems that the two brothers had come to terms with their past differences, with Lexel apologising for his poor behaviour. That was a poor sham which was not to last, as within the year Lexel helped himself to all the money in a joint account the two had opened, presumably in connection with monies due from the family interests or reparations. In due course Hansel tried to warn off his nephew, young Bolko who would in due course succeed to the titles, against having anything to do with Lexel, (Luke *Hansel Pless* p 238-9) but Bolko declined to get involved in such matters.

In 1970/71 Hansel and Mary divorced, but reasons are not given. This must have been as friendly an arrangement as his previous parting from Sissy, as the two of them continued to see a lot of each other over the ensuing years, almost on a daily basis.

Hansel continued to develop his idea for the seasoning of timber but the magic formula for real success seemed to elude him. His health had started to fail once he reached his eightieth birthday and many of his older friends and loyally supportive relations had already died. His Aunt Shelagh had passed on in 1970, at the age of 92. His own departure from this life in the end was quite sudden as he died in hospital on January 26th 1984.

He left his personal estate to Mary in recognition of the support and comfort she had given to him for nearly thirty years of his life. To her, supported by her family, fell the task of winding up his affairs and his business in Norfolk which had never really taken off, at least not as a really profitable commercial success.

Hansel's life had really been a strange one. Of the three sons of Hans and Daisy, he had perhaps been the one least attached to his mother and she seemed to have indulged him rather less than the younger Lexel and the sickly Bolko. Of course the First World War had almost removed him from Daisy's care in his teens as he was taken by his father to serve in his regiment, and he was apart from her during the whole of the war. Thereafter his period in Berlin studying had protracted the break as Daisy lived further away from him, and then her circumstances began to deteriorate.

Nevertheless, it was Hansel who set up and supported the

arrangements for Daisy in her later years and he selected her country, England, as the one in which he wished to live, although it was not to come about that she would join him.

He was cruelly rebuffed by that adopted country in the way he was held in custody for over three years, despite there being a lack of evidence of his being any risk to the country, at least none which would stand any close investigation. Even when the factors stated had been found to be invalid, it still became his lot to remain held on purely hypothetical grounds.

On the face of it, he had been cruelly treated by his own brothers, but no doubt there would be two sides to the story and it may be that the two younger brothers had reason to differ in their views as to how the family affairs should be run. However, that would not grant the right to the one remaining brother, Lexel, to misappropriate monies or other assets which formed part of the family estate.

From 1924, when his father had put Hansel in charge of the care of the family business affairs, that life had been a trial as he had to deal with the constant tussle between the family and the Polish government which followed the division of Silesia at the end of the 1914-18 War.

The gymnastics of the German economy added to the troubles. Pressure by his brothers, put on his father in his later years, which caused Hansel to be removed from the sole management of the family businesses, caused him great problems, especially when he succeeded as head of the family. These were to be with him for the rest of his life, even though the technical problem of management of the businesses was removed by the nationalisation of industry by the Poles after the Second World War.

Throughout all of this, especially when he was living in England he was supported by his uncle Bend'Or, Aunt Shelagh and his devoted cousin Ursula. The Westminsters certainly could not be faulted for their unwavering loyalty, and in the way they helped him both morally and financially.

His marriages, first to Sissy and then to Mary in later life were almost totally different. The first had given only a few happy years together before events were to separate them when Hansel left for England. Sissy, fearful of a strange country declined to follow him, yet they retained a strong bond for many years in their correspondence which still used terms of close endearment. Sissy continued to help and support him in his family troubles and in trying to see what was happening when Daisy died during the 1939-45 War years. Even in his long letter to Sissy after the war when he set out reasons for their separation, they were couched in terms which showed no rancour. Ever a gentleman, Hansel provided the grounds for her to divorce him. Sissy, born in August 1896 died in May 1994.

The marriage to Mary was also to break up but they continued to share close company, including visits to friends. It is not disclosed in Michael Luke's biography of Hansel just what brought about the marital break, but it was certainly not one of hatred, as can be the case in so many instances, and their mutual devotion seemed to be strongly evidenced right up until Hansel's death. Mary married again in 1997 to become Lady Mary Ashtown, wife of the seventh Baron.

The huge changes brought about by the social revolutions at the beginning of the 20th century which led to much bloodshed, and the dramatic intervention of the 1914-18 War had rocked the foundations of the noble families which had reigned supreme for many generations. More modest changes in the 'thirties' continued the move of power from the hands of the few into the clutches of the many, some of whom were ill qualified to be in control of such power.

The 1939-45 War interrupted the process as countries fought to retain what they thought was a right to mutual existence without oppression. The end of that conflict brought the final dismasting of the old rule as more moderate forces of modern socialism took firm root in many countries. The extremes of communism which then brought some dictatorships every bit as bad as the old tsarist rule also signalled the end of any further power being exercised by the rather sad remains of the old families.

For Hansel such changes must have been hard to bear but he did so with a remarkable pragmatism. Yes, he tried to fight to retain what was his, at least to secure for himself and his mother an income from assets which were being stripped away by events. He may have lost that fight for himself, but he lost neither his dignity nor his kind sensitivity for other people.

His story, as was that of his mother, Daisy, is a sad one, but it is a lesson in how strong personal fortitude can morally triumph over adversity, and for that, Hans Heinrich XVII, Count of Hochberg and 4th Prince of Pless should be remembered.

FOURTEEN

LEXEL

The second son of Hans, 3rd Prince of Pless, and his wife Daisy, was christened Alexander Frederick William George Conrad Ernest Maximilian, but fortunately was known familiarly as Lexel. He was born on 1st February 1905, in London. It is said that, as a child, he became his mother's favourite. He had the same fair hair as his mother and it is mentioned that during his early years she spent much of her time in dressing her son to suit his colouring. However, it is also remarked upon that Daisy was a disciplinarian and required her boys to do as they were told when they were told.

Daisy's eldest son Hansel was, as the heir to the family titles, keenly watched and guided by his father and, in essence, taken from her care in his mid teens to be trained as a soldier, later to serve in the 1914-18 War.

Daisy endeavoured to shelter the two younger ones, Lexel and Bolko, from the troubles of war in her own peripatetic lifestyle, as she moved home around war-torn Europe. Hansel records how Bolko complained to him that his mother gave most of her attention to Lexel. It is perhaps therefore not difficult to see how Lexel was to become a 'mother's boy' with a charming personality to the outside world, effeminate in his ways and carrying with him a make up box which he continued to do in his later life.

By the time he was a young man he had already fallen foul of authority as a result of a homosexual relationship. He was sentenced to two months gaol, but did not serve this as the accusation was half quashed by an appeal. One of the main witnesses committed suicide so, although no definitive act was proved, the Court still upheld the suspicion of an offence. This brush with the law for an offence, which was loathsome to a great number of people, and which was indeed illegal in those times, seriously affected relationships between the family and others.

Hans' second young wife Clotilde, whom he had married after his divorce from Daisy, did not wish to be associated with Lexel. Then later on, towards the end of the 1920s, Lexel's intended marriage to Princess Ileana of Rumania, which had been arranged by Daisy, was cancelled. This was as a result of the earlier scandal being dug up by the press and published for all to see. Hansel had previously told him that he should volunteer all his past to his potential in-laws but as Lexel did not do so, the sudden shock of this revelation was all the more dramatic for them.

Nothing further is mentioned in the family about this, but a book by L J Ludovici, *The Three of Us,* published in 1993, does cover his proclivity for associations of a like nature. This book also debates as to whether Lexel had fathered a child. He wrote a letter in 1948 saying how his illegitimate daughter had suddenly turned up to visit him. Ludovici also comments on the intimacy of his relationship with his half cousin, Ena Fitzpatrick, with whom his later life was to be so closely tied.

Little is disclosed about the early education of Lexel, or his brother Bolko, but they received lessons from private tutors. Insofar as Lexel was concerned the turnover of tutors was constant. What is known about Lexel, however, is that after his brush with the law he was packed off with a personal tutor to tour parts of the Middle East, a sort of mini Grand Tour which no doubt gave him a taste for such travels in his later life.

Those early travels, coupled with the subsequent, almost constant moving around with his mother during the First World War and the post war years, must have practised him well for the life he later led during and after the Second World War. He left France for England during the latter war and then, in the years afterwards, he travelled back to France and from France to Germany, to France again and finally to Majorca.

His childhood was one where he was lavished with attention by his mother, and although on the one hand she did not believe in spoiling her children, she nevertheless in the case of Lexel showered him with interest in all he did. His father looked to bring him up in the same manly disciplined way of his brother Hansel, with sport and outdoor gaming pursuits, but Lexel showed little interest, preferring to mix with his mother's friends.

Although Lexel hated the rough field sports of hunting and shooting, he was a natural nature lover for all of his life, extolling the merits of floral wildlife and he loved to journey on his own through forest and country.

Ena, short for Edwina, was Daisy's younger cousin and with another cousin, Olivia Countess of Larisch, they made a trio from the Irish Fitzpatrick family; they were all granddaughters of the Olivia who had been sent away from the London Court for her alleged dalliance with the Royal Prince Albert.

All three of them lived in Europe for most of their lives. Whereas Daisy and Olivia had married, Ena remained single. She first went to the continent in early 1914 at the age of twenty-one as a household companion to the Bopp family who lived in Schloss Mulhausen near Wurttemberg in South Germany. Caught there by the war, she stayed with them through the ensuing four years without any harassment from the authorities. However, that could not be said about her life at the Schloss as the entire male side of the family tried their hand at seducing the young Ena but they failed in their ambitions.

The first contact between Ena Fitzpatrick and Lexel was in 1916 when Ena visited Daisy at her house at Garmisch Partenkirchen in Bavaria. Lexel was only eleven and Ena was twenty three but the two of them seem from that moment to have captured a chord of understanding which developed into a lifelong attraction. It could well be that Ena, after suffering the continuous advances from the men in the Bopp family, found in Lexel a safe companion, but that does not account for the close attachment which they had for each other throughout the rest of their lives. There must have been another real emotional draw to bring them together. There were periods when they lived apart as Lexel took time now and then to indulge his fascination with young men but the connection remained to the end of their lives.

When Daisy and Hans divorced in 1922, Ena acted as Daisy's companion for a period until the end of October 1925 and this would have brought her into further contact with Lexel. As Ludovici says in *The Three of Us* regarding Ena and Lexel *'Their growing intimacy seems to have been consummated by 1924.'* Thereafter, for a time it seems that Ena must have acted as *chatelaine* at Fürstenstein before Hans re-married and subsequent contact would have been maintained and developed as Ena visited either Daisy or Lexel. Some years later, when Daisy had removed herself from Munich, she left the house to be lived in by Ena and Lexel.

Ena and Lexel lived together in the house during the 1930s but one event caused Ena to leave and find for herself some independent accommodation. She had been away and on returning to the house found Lexel and some male companions to be indulging in a gross homosexual orgy. This disgusted her and she severely upbraided him for his insensitivity in using his mother's house in that way. This rupture in their relationship lasted until shortly before 1939 when they had to flee Nazi Germany.

As has been recorded in the previous chapter, the burden of managing the affairs of the Pless estates fell on Hansel, as he was the eldest son. As Lexel grew older he conspired to gain that role for himself, at times being aided by his younger brother Bolko. (Luke, *Hansel Pless-Prisoner of History)*

Over the years Lexel tried to strip power away from Hansel in order to become the heir to his father's wealth and titles. In this he only partially succeeded, as although he gained control of the estates from Hansel at one time, it was a hollow achievement as by then the

Polish government was seeking their pound of flesh. The 1939-45 War brought German domination and afterwards, it was not long before Polish Communists nationalised the businesses. Lexel had gained no substantive control and he merely joined the queue in trying to obtain some compensation for the loss of the family businesses.

Hansel had more than once allowed himself to be taken in by Lexel's way of charming people, only to be at the receiving end of another plot. At one time Bolko joined Lexel against their older brother, plotting obscenely to persuade their father that Hansel should be removed from control of the family possessions. Between them they emptied Fürstenstein of many of its treasures and Lexel got his hands on Daisy's jewellery, some of which he used to fund his lifestyle in the rather romantic places where he chose to live. Lexel's life seemed to be reasonably filled with social enjoyment whereas Hansel lived in virtual poverty in London at one time.

The sequence of events is given by Michael Luke, beginning around 1934 when the Polish government began to put on pressure to get the legal control of the Pless estates, businesses and properties.

By then, Bolko who had married Clotilde, had run up considerable debts. He was also in the grip of drink and drugs. In order to get his elderly father, the Fürst, to pay his debts, he had attempted to blackmail him by making a statement that the Fürst had been complicit in the acts of Bolko and Clotilde when he, the Fürst, was still married to Clotilde. This false accusation appalled even Lexel and he managed to prevent the blackmail taking place.

However, Bolko then became involved with the Polish security forces to the extent that they persuaded him to visit Silesia where he was told that he should connive with Lexel to have Hansel removed from being the administrator of his father's estates as otherwise they would be declared bankrupt by the authorities; to cap the deal Lexel would be appointed in his stead. The plot included a threat to charge Hansel with perjury and have him arrested next time he came to Germany. At that time the country had an arrangement with the Poles which would have allowed this to happen. Hansel, when he later heard about this, considered it to be a definite threat to his life. It seems that Lexel was persuaded by Bolko to fall in with this plan.

The Polish authorities, in an attempt to gather in taxes, put their mark upon various properties and items at Pless, everything from pictures to the timber at the saw mills, and they seized money which was to be used to pay staff. Hansel and the Fürst decided that they would have to arrange to buy back any items auctioned off so as to be able to continue to pay their staff and keep affairs going.

Here the Fürst and Hansel had a difference of opinion; Hans did not trust Lexel but Hansel did and went to see him in Munich at his mother's house where Lexel was living at the time. He gave the money to Lexel to purchase the items but then it all went wrong for Hansel as Lexel passed the money to a lawyer who kept some of the money for himself, and then used the rest of it to lay a petition before a court on Lexel's behalf to appoint a guardian, other than Hansel, for the Pless estates. Lexel would then be able to withdraw a petition at the League of Nations, which was being made by Hansel against the sequestration of the estates by Poland.

Hansel re-visited his father, who admonished him for trusting his brother and they had to take legal action against both Lexel and Bolko.

It was the Nazi party who came to their aid, as at the time both the younger brothers were somewhat in thrall to them. They were reprimanded for their actions against their father. In due course Lexel at Fürstenstein admitted his part in the plot, during which Lexel confirmed that he and Bolko had written to authorities in Germany to the effect that Hansel was not suitable to manage the affairs of the estate, as he resided in England. Yet, even later, both the younger brothers attempted a connivance with the Nazis to get their father to hand over the estates. It was not successful.

Problems continued until 1936 when they were compounded by Hans' ill-health and then the arrest of Bolko on criminal charges followed by his death. Under pressure, the Fürst agreed eventually to make Lexel his attorney.

Hansel was called to Germany by the ailing and worried Hans in the last two years of his life, but the visits were not comfortable as Hansel was watched by Lexel and others, and was only granted very restricted access to Hans. When the Fürst eventually died in 1938 an agreement was reached by the lawyers as to the division of his estates between the two remaining brothers, Hansel and Lexel. At the end of this Hansel, for some reason, gave a power of attorney to Lexel, which was then abused.

When they met later in the post war years Lexel apologised for his behaviour but it was short lived as he took the money from a joint bank account they had set up on this occasion on what had seemed to be their reconciliation.

So much can be said for the relationships between the two brothers who had been born to great wealth and privilege. No doubt, just as Michael Luke has set out the case from Hansel's point of view in some detail, the same could be done for Lexel, but Ludovici's book is silent on the matter. Indeed, the latter in some ways confirms the shallow nature of Lexel's character in the acts of his later life, including his unreliability even to his cousin Ena with whom he had developed such a special relationship.

Matters concerning the two brothers' inter-relationships are described more in Michael Luke's book. Ludovici does not cover much of the immediate period after Lexel's childhood, touching only lightly on the intervening years before the outbreak of the 1939-45 War. He dwells more on the lives of Lexel and Ena after these earlier events and in conjunction with Margrit Willi and to a certain extent with Lexel's friend, Max.

There must certainly have been duplicity in Lexel's character as he turned against Hansel, as has already been seen, and also Ena at varying stages.

At the outbreak of the Second World War Lexel, Ena and others, after exiting from Warsaw in a great hurry, had taken shelter in a remote part of Southern France but it soon became obvious that they could not remain there.

Quite independently Lexel left to find his way to England, to be followed later by Ena, but thereafter their lives remained separate until the end of the war. Lexel had been born in London so he had British nationality as well as his adopted Polish, and he was to serve in the Polish units attached to the UK forces for the rest of the conflict. His places of service were as diverse as Scotland, the Polish military headquarters in London, North Africa, Egypt and Italy, where he took part in the assault at Monte Casino, although there is no other commentary available about his time in the army.

It is, perhaps, interesting to consider how people such as Lexel and Bolko, indeed Hansel's wife Sissy as well, were at first swayed in favour of the Nazi government in Germany, but were then to change, and in Lexel's case fight against them.

After the First World War, pressure by the French in the matter of reparations was the one significant fact which brought Germany to its economic knees. Hitler and his National Socialist Party came at a time when the people were looking for some inspired leadership to take a firm hold of the country and stand up for them against the French and others who were preventing Germany's recovery. The extremes of his regime soon became obvious to many who tried to defy the wickedness of his activities, and the torture chamber in Berlin bears witness to how many Germans were brutally treated and killed for their opposition to the Nazi regime. Consequent events in the Soviet zone and in other countries around the world have shown how the iron hand of a dictatorial regime can cow populations into submission.

At the end of the Second World War, Lexel and Ena met up once again in London where Ena had spent many of the war years in forms of service, such as being an ambulance driver, but for most of the time she was in the WRVS, which she endured rather than enjoyed.

The reunion was one which they both relished as Lexel set out for Europe in 1947 with Ena to recover a car which they had laid up in a garage at Marvejols near Paris. It was still there, just as it had been left, so the pair proceeded to Gorge du Tarn where they stayed in a chateau which had been converted into a hotel.

At the time, Lexel was largely dependent for income from an American friend, Charley Allen, who was working with Lexel on behalf of some other aristocrats who had claims for losses of their property and other interests in Silesia, such as Lexel's own claims. For his assistance Lexel received an honorarium of five hundred dollars a month, which must certainly have kept the wolf from the door.

Lexel had been cut out of Daisy's will as a result of all his manipulations but that did not stop him from taking possession of much of her jewellery, which in due course was given to Ena or sold.

1947 saw Lexel re-establishing himself in all his old haunts, and he took Ena with him. They ended up the year in Switzerland at Arosa, in the Pension Hotel. It was that they met Margrit Willi, the daughter of a Swiss plastic surgeon resident in London, who was to form a deep and lasting friendship with Ena.

In 1949 Lexel, taking Ena with him, travelled around parts of Europe but they returned to Arosa for the winter season once again. In the following year they headed south. After various pauses they came upon St Tropez, which took their fancy, and they eventually rented a small house, by name La Coccinelle, about two miles out of the town. It was there, that in general terms they were to live for the next four years, picking up new acquaintances and renewing some old ones.

One meeting was significant; in 1953 his old friend Charley Allen appeared and invited Lexel to set up a financial business with him in Frankfurt. As a result of this, quite suddenly Lexel announced that he would be leaving to live in Frankfurt despite his strong attachment to Ena, although he denied this when questioned by Magrit. From then on Margrit became Ena's constant companion and closest friend. In the end it was Margrit to whom Ena left her possessions in her will.

In Frankfurt, Lexel took up with Max, then but a teenager, and when Lexel was visited by Ena in 1954 she was shocked and realised that she would never again hold the same place in Lexel's affections. Lexel later adopted Max and he bestowed as much, if not more attention on him, than he had on Ena. This put a strain on the relationship between the two cousins and they did not live together again as a couple.

Despite this, Lexel continued to visit Ena in her various homes and he invited her to visit him over the years in his, but on more than one occasion he offended her sensitivities. A typical case concerned Max who was going to an important function with his wife. Lexel asked her to allow Max's wife to wear jewellery he had previously given to Ena, which had originally belonged to Daisy. Ena was very upset at this and refused to oblige him as she felt that the jewellery would vanish and she would have lost another part of the life which she held in dear remembrance.

On other occasions Lexel would say he would come to visit but then not arrive as promised. Ena would become anxious and excited at the thought of the visit, only to be let down by Lexel's selfishness in his arriving later and on one occasion not at all, usually just to suit him.

Lexel had let the house in which she lived for the season and kept the rents he received, leaving Ena to fend for herself, which she did by taking in paying guests and travelling around Europe visiting old friends. Lexel later left his flat in Frankfurt and moved in to the family home of his young companion, a situation which again caused his cousin much concern.

This new attachment did not prevent Lexel from demanding that Ena and Margrit, who had moved and taken up a new house to cater for their guests, should take in some of his friends as and when it suited him. For the next several years the group remained living apart, although Lexel visited about twice a year.

The social scenes of the 1920s and 30s were a shallow postscript of the Edwardian era and were only put aside for the Second World War but many of the disenfranchised aristocracy and other people of note survived to live in a sort of time warp around the Mediterranean Sea in the 1950s and 60s.

As the older ones died out they made way for the *nouveaux riche* of the post war era who had made fast money in various trade booms as the world righted itself and moved on from the restrictions of austerity Britain and Europe.

Lexel had the knack of appealing to these people, the older ones who were hanging on to the last vestiges of a bygone age, and the new ones who were attracted to a title to give some credence or substance to their hollow lives.

It is difficult to determine Lexel's financial situation over his life but it does seem that in 1970 he reached some agreement with Germany, having been granted nationality, which reportedly gave him ten million Deutschmarks as compensation for the loss of the Pless Estates. It appears that his ability to pay his way then did improve, although his offers of generosity were not always met by action.

In a significant move Lexel took up a house in Majorca and in due course that island became his main residence, as he purchased a large estate later with money, which presumably was from the compensation payment. He had great times on Majorca entertaining the important people in his life, and from time to time invited Ena and Margrit to stay. His attachment to Max was strong as ever and he took the young man and his wife with him as he visited his friends.

Lexel's financial state was never stable as he seemed to spend his money with relatively wild abandon. His desire to keep up with appearances amongst his circle of acquaintances and the money he must have spent on Max would have been a considerable burden and must have diminished his funds.

At some time in his later years Lexel also took to having facial surgery 'lifts' to maintain his looks. In addition, in London Hansel was taking legal action to obtain from him part of the compensation which Lexel had received from Germany.

The relationship he had with Max and his wife could be questioned as it was at times strained by the age difference. The tastes of the two men were quite opposite, Lexel with his retinue of distressed aristocracy and other older associates of the moment, the younger couple having their own age group of friends to consider. Ludovici illustrates this by quoting some of the exchanges between the two. Nevertheless, Max and his wife Anke conveniently put those differences aside and continued to accept the benefit of living with Lexel on Majorca.

On a different aspect it does seem that Lexel's extravagance with money and his constant desire to show off must have been an inferiority complex, which had been smouldering since childhood against his elder brother. Hansel was the natural heir to the Pless title and Lexel's efforts to have him removed in favour of himself must indicate the true nature of the relationship.

In 1972 he boasted to cousin Ena that he had used his mother's Fitzpatrick ancestry in order to get Irish nationality in the name of Count Alexander Hochberg. This gave him a great deal of satisfaction as the Germans and British only called him 'Mr'. As Michael Luke says in his book, the month after Hansel died must have given Lexel some final satisfaction that he held the title Prince of Pless, even if only for such a short period, before he too left for higher places.

It was fortunate for Ena that Margrit Willi had succeeded to her father's entire estate when he died in 1971. That came to several million Swiss Francs and it made it possible for the two of them to live in comfort. No money came from Lexel to support his cousin Ena; an allowance of 700 Deutschmark a month which he had offered was never forthcoming, although he had previously paid some medical bills on her behalf.

The two cousins, Lexel and Ena lived on through the 1970s with occasional visits to each other but whatever pleasures and jollity there had been in their past relationship had gone as by then they both had become increasingly disabled, Ena especially, who had to rely on her by then devoted friend Margrit for everything.

The end was quite sudden; Hansel died on the 23rd January 1984 in England, Lexel on the 22nd of February and his cousin Ena had preceded him to the grave by three days. So within one month three of the people who had been closest to Daisy all passed away; as brother Bolko had died in 1936 that brought to an end a complete phase in the life of the original Cornwallis-West family.

Insofar as the Hochberg and Pless family was concerned the title passed to the nephew Bolko, the son of the short lived marriage between the brother Bolko who had died young and Clotilde, the second wife of Daisy's husband.

FIFTEEN
BOLKO

The third child of Hans and Daisy was born in Berlin on 23rd September 1910 and christened Bolko Conrad Friedrich. Bolko was not only the name of his uncle but also of an ancestor on his father's side. It was an extremely difficult birth for both mother and son and contrary to medical expectations Bolko survived into his teenage years but he remained a sickly child whose subsequent health as a young adult was never good. He died in 1936.

His mother's health was also affected by the birth; in fact she was so ill she was not expected to live. This trauma probably triggered the series of ailments which were to trouble her throughout the rest of her life.

Unlike his brothers, no specific biography has been written about Bolko, so most of the information which follows has been garnered from publications about his mother and Hansel and Lexel; all these sources are referred to in the bibliography. Most notably, Michael Luke, in his book *Hansel Pless – Prisoner of History* covers a number of matters about Bolko's later years which are referred to below.

In an attempt to obtain direct comment, both the author and the author's daughter, who lives not far from Munich, have made contact by telephone with a gentleman at an address in that city given as that of Bolko Graf von Hochberg und Fürst Von Pless.

The author's daughter was told that that there had been no contact with the Cornwallis-West family for over fifty years.

Shortly afterwards the author enquired if there were likely to be any photographs of the three brothers, Daisy's sons, but was told very politely by the gentleman that it was a long time ago and he 'had nothing to do with the family' and so the connection has not been pursued any further.

Any comments made about Bolko's life and his alleged behaviour are therefore based on observations by the other authors.

Although the two younger boys spent their childhood more with Daisy than their father, Bolko saw less of his mother during the First World War as she carried out her nursing duties and therefore much of his upbringing would have been at the hands of staff or tutors. This meant that he was in some ways a stranger to Daisy, and he later on commented on this to his older brother, Lexel.

Little is recorded about his teenage years, but what is known is that when Bolko was fifteen he was living with his father who by then had re-married. Clotilde, Bolko's stepmother was fourteen years older than him and over forty years younger than her new husband. Bolko had sufficient fire in his blood, so it would seem, to carry on a liaison with Clotilde.

The affair continued and over time scandal grew until at one point it seemed likely that criminal proceedings would arise against Bolko's father, the Fürst, because of his possible connivance at what was a crime. Shortly afterwards proceedings for the annulment of the marriage began. Bolko and Clotilde moved away to live in Munich and they married in July 1934 after Clotilde's marriage with Hans had been annulled.

For some years Bolko had been a keen supporter of the Nazi principles, both he and Clotilde being on very close terms with high ranking officials in the movement. Unlike Lexel who toyed with the ideals and became quite active before turning from them in the early 1930s, Bolko remained involved.

Bolko had also become addicted to alcohol and drugs and this led him into debt. His personality changed from that of a pleasant young man to one bearing a grudge and this was to emerge against his father.

He put together a document which said that his father had been compliant in Bolko's liaison with his, then, wife Clotilde and he planned to blackmail Hans to pay off his debts. This plan was frustrated by his two older brothers.

To compound this first felony, Bolko then connived with the Polish government, assisting them in their plans to get control of the Pless estates and away from the hands of his father and eldest brother Hansel who was the appointed administrator.

Because of this scheming and similar action by Lexel, Daisy took both Lexel and Bolko out of her will and made Hansel the sole beneficiary. That was really almost symbolic as by the time she died, Daisy was penniless and much of her jewellery had been pawned to provide for her upkeep.

The machinations of the two younger brothers, especially that of Bolko brought them to the attention of the authorities and Bolko ended up in gaol. Although a move to another prison had been arranged, he was released instead. Michael Luke comments in his book that this was probably due to bribes being paid.

On his release from prison, Bolko went home to Pless where it is suggested that despite being warned off alcohol due to his medical condition, he drank copiously, resulting in his death in June 1936.

It was also suggested that Lexel and his money-lending schemer, Grunwald, had allowed drink to be made available to Bolko while at the same time promoting the idea to the Fürst that Hansel was responsible for his imprisonment. This was all part of a plot to discredit Hansel and be rid of Bolko who had become a liability. Whatever the case may have been, Bolko, having been complicit in both the plots against Hansel and his father, was now out of the way, leaving Lexel to manipulate his way to his own ends.

In his marriage to Clotilde, Bolko had fathered three children, two daughters and a son, also called Bolko, who was born on 3rd April 1936. This was shortly before Bolko senior's death on 22nd June of that year.

Although Hans, the old Fürst, had originally married Clotilde, their son Konrad, born on 12th June 1930, had died on 29th November 1934. Therefore the inherited titles passed to young Bolko, technically the grandson of the old Fürst, and the nephew of the two other brothers, Hansel and Lexel, after their deaths.

Thus in 1984 Bolko took all the titles as Count of Hochberg, Baron of Fürstenstein and 6th Fürst von Pless, or Prince of Pless, and made his home in Munich.

His sisters, the daughters of Clotilde and Bolko, by then were living in London and Germany, thus perhaps reflecting the bipartite nature of the family of which they are descendants.

This 6th Prince of Pless married in 1964 and in 1965 had one daughter, but then divorced in 1969, and as noted above, he lives in Munich.

The very extensive genealogy of the Hochberg family shows two other males named Hans Heinrich (XX and XXI respectively) with a note alongside each saying 'renounced succession rights'.

It is not the point of this exercise to explore the Hochberg (Pless) family, so the matter will rest there.

CONCLUSION

That is the end of the story we wish to pursue. There are more avenues of related descendants, notably those emanating from the marriage of Shelagh to Bend'Or, 2nd Duke of Westminster, and by any consequential issue of the daughters of the second marriage of Hans, 3rd Prince of Pless to Clotilde, and of course the issue of the present 6th Prince of Pless, Bolko, but they are not for these pages.

We shall draw a veil over the possibilities of any consequent issue of Lexel from the illegitimate daughter he suddenly paraded in his later years, nor venture down any path which may relate to the alleged dalliances of Edward, Prince of Wales so many years ago.

The parentage of the various participants in this family story has caused various writers to express views which may or may not be without foundation.

George Cornwallis-West observed of the Admiral in his book *The Life and Letters of Admiral Cornwallis* that in his latter years he might have married the young widow of Captain Whitby. However, as he points out, the relationship between the two had always seemed to be one of surrogate father and daughter, indeed that the Admiral had regarded John Whitby as the son he never had.

In pure terms the last comment could be disputed, as in the Cornwallis Family History there is a comprehensive list of allegedly bastard descendants of the Admiral amongst the local population from his days as a young officer serving in the West Indies station. This appeared in those times to be the almost legitimate, but certainly accepted relief from the many frustrations of virile young officers on board ship and away from their homes and families for months on end.

The Whitbys' daughter, Theresa, undoubtedly was regarded by the Admiral as his surrogate granddaughter, and in due course she was the joint founding partner of the new family by marrying the De La Warr grandson, Frederick West. There was no doubt ever cast upon the legitimacy of their offspring.

Thereafter it gets a trifle more complicated. First, in Ridley's book on Bend'Or, Duke of Westminster, it is commented that young William, Theresa and Frederick's son, in his sojourn in Florence had fathered three daughters; but then on his return to Britain and his marriage to Patsy other writers express various opinions about the rumours which circulated about the parentage of their offspring. In his book *Patsy*, Tim Coates implies quite strongly that at least George was the son of Edward, Prince of Wales.

In their book about the Churchill boys, *Winston and Jack*, the authors, Celia and John Lee are bolder, indeed commenting (p218) that *'Daisy ... was one of the Prince's favourite daughters'* amongst his various attributed progeny. Taking that as the extreme case, one might enquire why William on taking Patsy, one of the most beautiful women of the day as his wife, had not fathered the children who lived with them as their family. If the statements made by Ridley about the daughters in Florence are true, it can not have been down to any lack of ability to be a normal biological father.

He certainly can not have been bought off by the Prince as the family financial estates were never very healthy under his care, and he received no titles as any reward for 'turning his back' on the alleged and widely rumoured affair between the Prince and Patsy. There are no further imputations of other illegitimate offspring being raised as a result of William's activities away from home. It would be unfair to suggest there may have been a private birth rate amongst the young women of the district as writers are silent on such matters. Perhaps even more curiously, as Patsy is said to have been the lover of the Prince since the age of sixteen, there is no mention of any consequent results out of wedlock, only those after her marriage being subject to this questioning.

Therefore, as has been commented in the individual chapters, it is unwise to be definite in these matters, it being sufficient to say that there are some grounds to be sceptical about the various claims and counter claims made by writers. That is not to dispute the validity of any of their observations, other than for such to be evidenced by actual authentic documents which would support any expressions of opinion.

Amongst the three children, the circumstances of whose birth are surrounded by the foregoing mysteries, are concerned, there is no suggestion that their offspring are anything other than the direct and legitimate children of their marriages. The children of Daisy and Shelagh are under absolutely no shadow of doubt as to their parentage, and George had no children. Books about his first wife, Jennie, do suggest that he had indulged in some sexual philandering from time to time but no comment is made about any results thereof. Even Daisy's unrequited loves described by Koch and set out in her diaries are clear that they never strayed beyond strong emotional feelings and without physical attachment.

The nearest one then gets to any further developments in this quarter is the affair between Bolko and his father's second wife, and then the rather curious claim that Lexel had given birth to a daughter at some time in his younger years, this being despite his well-known interest in those of his own sex. Any attachment that Lexel had for his cousin Ena seems to have been without anything other than their close relationship, although it seems that any hidden passion may have been more from Ena to Lexel than the other way around. In the later years of their relationship it was Lexel who moved away to live with his younger friends and only visited Ena as it suited him.

With the remarks concerning the various observations made in the literature available, it is clear that these questions will continue to fascinate those who have an interest in such matters.

My purpose in writing this book was to bring to light in the 21st century a little bit of history which centred around the times of the huge social changes in European society, encapsulated within the years from the late 19th century, through the period during and in-between the two world wars and into the post war era.

In summary, the lifetime of the participants spans from the year of 1744 when William, later the Admiral, was born, until 1984 when the last of the three sons of Daisy died. During that period the power which had rested amongst Kings, Queens and Emperors was lost, and control of events moved to those who had either seized power by force or were elected by the people.

The first Great War was undoubtedly a child of the Imperial dynasties as they squabbled over their territorial boundaries. Only twenty five years later the second major conflict was, at least in Europe, brought about by a dictator who had seized control of a country at a convenient time when its people were in real despair through poverty, but who then set about oppressing minorities. In consequential years the differences, which is supposed to be progress, between kingly rule and some subsequent regimes in other countries have echoed uncomfortable similarities to the latter conflict.

The politicians had the final say, but they were nevertheless in the main, and certainly in the latter part of the 19th century, still drawn largely from the upper classes. Connections with the nobility were commonplace so it was likely that aristocratic families would still be in a position to communicate either directly or indirectly with ministers. Government cabinets were full of the eminent and titled. Despite the power of government having moved from Crown to Parliament in former centuries, the influence of the monarch of the time was not insignificant. As, for about half a century, the Prince of Wales had been circulating in the same circles, he would be equally familiar with people in important positions.

The marked exception to this rule was Russia and the other countries which ultimately formed the Soviet bloc. Certainly in the former, considerable blood was spilt as those aristocrats connected with the Tsarist regime lost their heads, and the relatively few who did not suffer that fate departed the country for obscure retirement.

The position was even more tied to old aristocratic and titled families in Germany up to the Revolution in 1918, as those families were the rocks on which Bismarck had founded the German nation in 1871. Of course, the marital links between Queen Victoria's children and various German Royal families strengthened this bastion of old families with influences in both Britain and Germany, in some cases the many connections then made exist into present times.

Daisy was not the only one affected by the Great War with a conflict of loyalties; the Kaiser's own mother was Queen Victoria's daughter. Further, Queen Victoria's grandson by Prince Leopold, Duke of Albany was Prince Charles Edward, Earl of Clarence who was married off to yet another German dynasty. He actively supported Germany and was therefore a controversial figure in Britain due to his status as Sovereign Duke of Saxe-Coburg and Gotha. George V, in an effort to distance his dynasty from its German origins, changed the name of the British Royal Family from the House of Saxe-Coburg and Gotha to the House of Windsor and deprived Charles of his British peerages and honours and the title Prince.

In the years following the First World War large numbers of these disenfranchised families were left to pick up the pieces of their former lives, many to lead a semi-gentrified existence wandering Europe in a shiftless fashion. The Second World War virtually killed that off; those remaining were very often elderly inhabitants of the various spa towns and resorts on the continent or on Mediterranean islands where they chose to reside.

The span of the Cornwallis-West family is typical of the era, starting with William the Admiral who held a seat in Parliament before the Reform Act. His family had one in its gift and the one he chose to contest, Portsmouth, was a 'naval' seat. After his election William was a non-active participant in the House.

His brother, Charles, had previously held the sinecure of the 'family' seat of Ely, Suffolk, and his brother James was Bishop of Lichfield and Coventry, a position as much due to influence in high places as to ecclesiastical effort.

The first to carry the name Cornwallis-West, as a result of the marriage of his mother into an old titled family, was also a William. He was fairly soon gifted with the trappings of office, as the Lord Lieutenant of his County, the Honorary Colonel of the local county Regiment, and as a Member of Parliament.

His wife, Patsy, took advantage of the connections she made via her friendship with the Prince and the social activities within his circle. In the end her manipulations were to be her downfall.

The two daughters of the marriage of William and Patsy were to be the beneficiaries as in both cases they were married off to two of the most powerful families in Europe – Shelagh in England to the Grosvenors and Daisy in Germany to the House of Pless.

The son George was to find his own way in society but he was hooked by, or gained by himself (which ever way you are inclined to interpret the evidence) the hand of the mother of the man who was to be Britain's most famous Prime Minister. Jennie (Lady Churchill) in her own right was from a wealthy and influential American family; and her later connections in England through her marriage into a leading noble family with a son who developed into a notable politician brought her the power of connections which she ruthlessly exploited.

However, Jennie's talent for going through money and living in a style which she could not afford was not one to help George in balancing his budgets. Between the two of them they exceeded their income by substantial margins; for much of their lifetime loans or guarantees needed to be extended to them.

The lives of these people illustrate the huge change in fortunes experienced during the 20th century.

The pages of George's *Edwardian Hey-Days* show a classic example of the period, a cross between the grace and favour of the declining years of the aristocracy then sliding into comparative poverty, or at least very much straightened circumstances, of his latter years in rooms in a seaside resort.

This is also reflected in the biography of Hansel Pless, Daisy's eldest son who despite being of German birth and fighting for that country in the first Great War, then acquired Polish nationality and preferred to live in England, receiving naturalisation in 1947, calling himself simply, Mr Pless.

Hansel's lifestyle was modest at best, yet he retained the comfort of connections with many people of influence, although these could not save him from his three years of confinement as an alien during the Second World War.

The life of Daisy shows even more dramatically the fall from a position of power. She, who had been intimate in the circles of the Prince of Wales and the German Emperor, was left in the end to live on almost nothing and in very poor health, assisted only by dedicated companions and the kindness of local trades people, as at times she did not have even the money to pay for food.

Daisy's second son, Lexel, had a life which encapsulated the way the people in power changed from being amongst the aristocracy to others of more humble birth who rose to become the champions of the people. The revolutions in Europe which removed many royal rulers began when he was a child and the change continued during his life. It cannot be said that in all cases this brought a much better government as too many of the new elite chose to take as much from the state, in fact even more in many cases, than those whom they had usurped.

Those of high birth who did not meet a violent end in the early stages of some revolutionary conflicts escaped into exile. In the less violent changes of power some remained in their birth countries as rather nondescript ordinary citizens living modest lives, very often working in order to raise the money to keep body and soul sustained. Others moved into a peripatetic lifestyle, divided between home connections and sheltering in countries with less strained regimes.

Lexel tended to be amongst this latter group of semi-evacuees although it is not on record that he soiled his hands with honest work when funds were tight.

Hansel lived a more genteel life, certainly in the way he kept up a modest social life with his various relations and friends, despite the extreme poverty in which he lived for quite a while. He did try to keep himself usefully employed with the experimental work in trying to find a new timber preserving process, but it was not employment which brought him much, if any, income.

Both brothers and their Uncle George demonstrated the lifestyles which were typical of the semi-disowned aristocracy in the period between the two world wars and after the second conflict in their different ways. They were the last of an era both in habits and courtesies, as the rampant commercialism of modern life has ruthlessly taken over.

Privilege these days is almost entirely the prerogative of the cash-rich, who can be anyone from successful business people to pop stars or sports personalities, although democratically elected leaders now seem to have acquired their own idea of parliamentary elitism, as the cost of the regimes which bear upon the people is possibly far greater than the much criticised privileges of the former royal houses.

From amongst the Cornwallis-West family the most interesting person in many ways was Daisy. Here was an individual born into privilege, who by marriage was to be able to live a life of luxury which she plainly enjoyed. Yet on the other hand, she rebelled against its strictures, certainly the ones which pertained in Germany. Despite this she was determined to use the connections she enjoyed quite ruthlessly to get what she needed, most notably in her social and her charitable work. One is given the impression that she might have been treated generously in that regard, if only to get her off the backs of the parties she was lobbying.

Certainly, if the biographers are to be believed, and there is no reason to doubt them, Daisy became highly regarded by the ordinary people of the country around Fürstenstein, Waldenberg and Pless, as she fought to improve the living conditions of the workers' families which were quite appalling. The way in which she set about providing work for the lace makers, who had been ripped off by exploiting middlemen for years, was quite remarkable too.

In a way, these works put Daisy in a similar position to Florence Nightingale, although that comparison may not be quite as incongruous as it may seem, as Daisy also nursed the sick soldiers during the First World War.

However, like most of the displaced nobility, Daisy was to end up bereft of funds and apart from a few and very occasional family visitors, she was isolated from the society of which she had been a sparkling part for so many years.

Daisy's husband, Hans the Prince of Pless, who had been so notable in German society during the first quarter of the 20th century, became a relict of former times, much dependant on his sons for support but with Lexel and Bolko both scheming against him and Hansel at times and manipulating the family affairs to suit their own needs.

Any power which Hans might have had within the upper levels

of German or Polish society went with the Kaiser's abdication. The new political regimes had no use for him and the family fortunes became a target for the states to argue over. In his later years he appeared to be a greatly saddened man, as not only were his sons fighting over any inheritance but his second wife left him to take up with his youngest son, with whom she plainly had been consorting for some time in the family home.

Although the earlier years of the families were full of joy, the marriages, other than Theresa Whitby's to Frederick West and Patsy's to William, were not long lasting. Even Lexel's relationship with his cousin, Ena, was marked by tensions, as he left her for his young lovers, playing fast and loose with her undoubted devotion to him.

As one considers the lives of the family and their misfortunes, it seems almost as if a curse had been laid upon them. Even Jennie had an untimely end. She broke her ankle, gangrene set in and most of one leg had to be amputated. She had a haemorrhage and died at the not old age of sixty seven.

It is thus, when reading about the various characters in the Cornwallis-West family, that one cannot remain untouched by an element of sadness, starting with the lonely life of the Admiral in his singular attachment to the Navy and the two young people with whom he became so friendly, and who were, unwittingly, to be the seed corn for the Cornwallis-West family story to unfold.

Whatever their position in the society of those days, they were people who had to make huge adjustments as the years progressed. It was the fate of all the leading characters in this family story, with the exception of the Duchess of Westminster, Shelagh, to be stripped of their ornaments of prestige, especially wealth. The titles remained as a remembrance of better times for them, but the way in which they had been able to live their lives was gone for ever.

EPILOGUE

The main houses associated with the Cornwallis-West family were at Ruthin in Wales and Newlands in Hampshire. There was also a London town house at 42, Eaton Place.

Through the marriages of the daughters Daisy and Shelagh, the historical houses of the Westminsters at Eaton Hall in Cheshire and at Grosvenor Place in London, and the castles at Fürstenstein, Pless and Waldenberg in Silesia became associated with them.

However, this book is only concerned with the first two major named residences where the Cornwallis-West family was raised and lived. These houses at Ruthin and Newlands Manor, both edifices of the 19th century other than the original castle ruins at Ruthin, are still in use in the 21st century.

It is perhaps somewhat ironic that the original and historical Cornwallis family seat at Brome in Suffolk was demolished in the 1960s after some years of neglect, although the subsequent family seat of Culford Hall, also in Suffolk, survives as an independent school. It had been sold on the death of the 2nd Marquis Cornwallis in 1823, as he had been less than careful with the family money.

Likewise, the fairly ancient Creswell Hall in Staffordshire, the birthplace of John Whitby who can be regarded as one of the originators of the Cornwallis-West family, was demolished after being in the hands of other families for several years.

It is sad that the properties and acquired wealth which had been the reward of the state to the two brothers, one a noted General and the other the Admiral mentioned in these pages, should have met the same fate due to the careless attitude to money by their heirs, though in the latter case of the Admiral his not being by bloodline. Thankfully some items have survived within extensions of the Cornwallis family down the female line through their marriages into other families.

Of the brothers, General Charles Cornwallis has a fair number of portraits hung in a variety of locations, not just in England, but around the world, whereas his brother Admiral William is less well recorded. In fact he seems almost to have avoided being the subject of the artist's brush, which seems to match the modesty which was his normal demeanour.

Indeed, such was his reticence to be praised for his efforts that the Admiral refused to accept recognition for some of his very courageous naval actions, the famous, much praised and tactically exemplary 'Retreat' being one notable example. Only three years before his death he was finally persuaded to accept the GCB but the irony then was that he was too ill to actually receive the honour from the Sovereign before he died.

Readers who may be interested in learning more about the original family up to the present day should obtain a copy of *The Cornwallis Family History* published by Quacks Publishers of York in 2006 on behalf of the 3rd Baron Cornwallis.

BIBLIOGRAPHY

Although there are mentions of some of the characters of the Cornwallis-West family in various places amongst other literature, my main sources of reference, including those for the Cornwallis family have been: –

The Cornwallis Family History, published by the 3rd Baron Cornwallis, The Reverend N B Cryer and Quacks Publishers of York, 2006.

The Life and Letters of Admiral Cornwallis, compiled and written by George Cornwallis-West, published by Robert Holden & Co Ltd., London, 1927.

Edwardian Hey-Days, written by George Cornwallis-West, published by G B Putman's and Sons, London & New York, 1930.

Precursors of Nelson, compilation of essays by Peter le Fevre and Richard Harding, *Sir William Cornwallis,* written by Andrew Lambert, published by Chatham Publishing of London, 2000.

Nelson, The New Letters, edited by Colin White, published by The Boydell Press of Woodbridge, Suffolk. 2005.

Trafalgar, Countdown to Battle, written by Alan Schom, published by Michael Joseph of London, 1990.

Fortunes Daughters, written by Elisabeth Kehoe, published by Atlantic Books of London, 2004.

Perfect Darling, written by Eileen Quelch, published by Cecil and Amelia Woolf of London, 1972.

Daisy, Princess of Pless, written by W John Koch, published by W John Koch Publishing of Canada, 2005.

Patsy, The Story of Mary Cornwallis-West, written by Tim Coates, published by Bloomsbury Publishing plc of London, 2003.

Hansel Pless, Prisoner of History, written by Michael Luke, published by the Cygnet Press, London, 2001.

The Three of Us, written by L J Ludovici, published by Marjay Books of London, 1993.

Bend'Or, 2nd Duke of Westminster, written by George Ridley, published by Robin Clark Ltd, London, 1985.

Dark Lady, written by Charles Higham, published by Virgin Books Ltd of London, 2006.

Winston and Jack, The Churchill Brothers, both written and published by Celia and John Lee, 2007.

History of the County of Hampshire Volume 5, 1912.

The Parish Records of St Mary, Stafford by courtesy of the Staffordshire Record Office.

By the kindness of the Milford-on-Sea Historical Record Society, the following have been made available to view:

Milford House, by Joanna K Coldicott.

Country Houses around Lymington, Brockenhurst and Milford-on-Sea, published by Blake Pinnell.

From the Society's own *Occasional Magazine* publications:

Silk Production at Milford, by Agatha Harris (1917)

Notes on the older houses of Milford, (1924)

The Making of Mrs Whitby, by Mary Trehearne M.A. (1982)

The Story of Newlands Manor, by Jean Macdonald (2004)

A History of the Educational Facilities in the Milford Area 1660-1948, by Jeremy Greenwood (2004)

The author recognises the authors and publishers of these books and literature and is grateful for the information therein which has assisted in the compilation of this work. Of course this book about members of the Cornwallis-West family only covers some of the main facts about their lives; the biographies listed above are far more comprehensive. Any readers who are interested in furthering their knowledge about this fascinating group of people are recommended to seek out these original works.

PICTURE ACKNOWLEDGEMENTS

Muzeum Zamkowe w Pszczynie, Poland:
Page 62 (bottom left) & p.102 Daisy of Pless, Lafayette Studio, London 02.09.1898 MP/Psz/673
Page 107 Hans Heinrich XV von Hochberg, c. 1908 reproduction from book *Fürstenstein 1509-1909* by E. Zivier published in 1909 in Kattowitz (Katowice) MP/Psz/672
Page 117 Hans Heinrich XI von Hochberg, Johannes TATZELT, Waldenburg in Schlesien, 1905 MP/Psz/664
Page 127 Daisy in Red Cross uniform, E. Walsleben, pastel on cardboard, Breslau 1916 MP/Psz/3
Page 147, 148 Hans Heinrich XVII von Hochberg, E. Bieber, c.1930 MP/Psz/697

Milford-on-Sea Historical Record Society:
Page 54 photo, Page 104 Daisy Cornwallis-West from a painting by Reginald Arthur

National Portrait Gallery, London:
Page 62, 82 George F.M. Cornwallis-West by Henry H. Walter Barnett NPG x45264

Staffordshire County Council:
Page 31 Cresswell Hall

Alan Chapple:
Pages 38, 39, 60

3rd Baron Cornwallis:
Pages 10, 11, back cover from a painting of Admiral Sir William Cornwallis-West by R. Gardner

Henry Hornyold-Strickland Esq.
Pages 10, 33 Capt. John Whitby from a painting by J. Hoppner
Pages 10, 40 Theresa Whitby from a painting by J. Hoppner

W. John Koch:
Pages 146, 147 (bottom left and right), 167, 179

Anthony Saint Claire, Chairman, Countrypark Hotels Ltd:
Page 50 and front cover, picture Ruthin Castle
Pages 61, 63 William Cornwallis-West from a painting (artist unknown)
Pages 61, 70 Patsy Cornwallis-West from a painting (artist unknown)

Shelagh Cornwallis-West:
Page 139 from a private collection

Mrs Frederick West:
Page 10, 51 from a painting by an unknown artist

Illustrations from the author's collection: Pages 4, 9, 47, 81, 108, 141, 144

Illustrations from the publisher's collection: Pages 8, 54, 55, 64, 71, 73, front cover